Mestizo Worship

A Pastoral Approach to Liturgical Ministry

Virgilio P. Elizondo
and
Timothy M. Matovina

A Liturgical Press Book

 THE LITURGICAL PRESS
Collegeville, Minnesota

Cover design by David Manahan, O.S.B. Cover photo: Our Lady of Guadalupe feast day celebration, San Fernando Cathedral, San Antonio, Texas. Courtesy Manuel Medellin.

Acknowledgments

Acknowledgment is gratefully made to the following publishers for permission to use already published material: Orbis Press (Maryknoll, N.Y.) for "Living Faith: Resistance and Survival," by Virgilio P. Elizondo, *Galilean Journey: The Mexican-American Promise* (1983) 32-46; T. & T. Clark (Edinburgh) for "Popular Religion as Support of Identity: A Pastoral-Psychological Case-Study Based on the Mexican American Experience in the USA," by Virgilio P. Elizondo, *Popular Religion*, ed. Norbert Greinacher and Norbert Mette, *Concilium* 186 (1986) 36-43; Seabury (New York) for "Our Lady of Guadalupe as a Cultural Symbol: 'The Power of the Powerless,'" by Virgilio P. Elizondo, *Liturgy and Cultural Religious Traditions*, ed. Herman Schmidt and David Power, *Concilium* 102 (1977) 25-33; "Our Lady of Guadalupe Celebrations in San Antonio, Texas, 1840-41," by Timothy M. Matovina, *Journal of Hispanic/Latino Theology* 1 (November 1993) 77-96; "The Treasure of Hispanic Faith," by Virgilio P. Elizondo, *Origins* 10 (11 September 1980) 203-208; "Liturgy, Popular Rites, and Popular Spirituality," by Timothy M. Matovina, *Worship* 63 (July 1989) 351-361; "Marriage Celebrations in Mexican American Communities," by Timothy M. Matovina, *Liturgical Ministry* 5 (Winter 1996) 22-26.

1   2   3   4   5   6   7   8

Library of Congress Cataloging-in-Publication Data

Elizondo, Virgilio P.
   Mestizo worship : a pastoral approach to liturgical ministry /
Virgilio P. Elizondo and Timothy M. Matovina.
         p.   cm.
   Includes bibliographical references.
   ISBN 0-8146-2490-1 (alk. paper)
   1. Mexican American Catholics.   I. Matovina, Timothy M., 1955– .
II. Title.
BX1407.M48E57   1998
282—dc21   97-52052
                                                            CIP

Contents

Preface

At San Fernando Cathedral in San Antonio, Texas, a vital tradition among the primarily Mexican-American congregation is a Good Friday passion drama. The youth and other parishioners lead this liturgy, which begins in the public market, winds through the city's downtown streets, and ends with the crucifixion on the steps of the cathedral.

During one such procession, from among the thousands gathered, a three-year-old child spontaneously stepped forward to wipe the face of Jesus. This child's act of compassion reflects Archbishop Arthur J. Drossaerts' comments on Mexican-American religious practice nearly seventy years ago. Impressed by the devotion he observed, Drossaerts wrote of Mexican-descent Catholics at San Antonio:

> The great feasts of the Church do not only commemorate for them the wonders of God's love and mercy; no, they bring the great events of Christ's life and of His saints to the very doors of their hearts. In their vivid imagination Christ, lying in the cold manger of Bethlehem, or Christ hanging bruised and bleeding on the cross, is present before them: they see Him; they hear Him; they touch Him; they speak with Him (letter to American Board of Catholic Missions, 1929).

Like the aforementioned compassionate gesture of a modern-day Veronica at San Fernando parish, Drossaerts' statement reveals that Mexican-American expressions of faith are a treasured means of encountering God in worship. This book examines Mexican-American foundational faith expressions, particularly Our Lady of Guadalupe, as a sacred encounter with the God who accompanies the people in their historical and contemporary experience. While immediately applicable to ministry with Mexican Americans and other Latinos, this volume also offers helpful insights for anyone who celebrates the sacred in communities with worship traditions different from their own. In our experience, such communities provide a graced opportunity for liturgists and other pastoral agents to encounter Christ in the faith expressions of the people they serve.

The genesis of this book is our collaboration on the San Fernando Cathedral Study, a project conducted by the Mexican American Cultural Center in San Antonio and funded by the Lilly Endowment. Our conversations and work sessions during that study inspired us to integrate these previously published essays into a single volume.

This book stems from an ongoing dialogue between a Mexican-American pastor and an Irish-Croatian American who learned Spanish and began pastoral ministry with Mexican Americans as an adult. We enjoy working together and find that our "insider" and "outsider" perspectives enrich one another. Besides our pastoral experience, our collaborative effort also draws on our study and discussions of theology, culture, anthropology, ritual studies, liturgy, and history.

We are grateful to the Lilly Endowment for supporting the San Fernando Study and for providing us the opportunity to deepen our working relationship and friendship. In particular, we thank Olga Villa Parra, James P. Wind, Craig Dykstra, Jeanne Knoerle, and Carol Johnston for their expertise and encouragement. Our colleagues at the Mexican American Cultural Center also supported our efforts, especially Enedina P. Cardona, Rosendo Urrabazo, María Elena González, Roberto Piña, Rosa María Icaza, John Linskens, Jane Hotstream, Janie Dillard, and Lupe Ruiz. Other colleagues offered valuable comments on various parts of this manuscript; these include Arturo Pérez Rodríguez, Jake Empereur, Martha Ann Kirk, Charles Acree, Jacques Audinet, Chris Megargee, Margaret Mary Kelleher, Lizette Larson Miller, Jaime R. Vidal, and Raúl Gómez. Elida Yañez helped with the final editing of the book. Angel Mena assisted us with his computer expertise on this and various other projects. Above all, we are grateful to the people of San Fernando Cathedral who have animated our faith and theological reflection.

V.P.E.
T.M.M.

PART ONE

Foundational Faith
Expressions

Introduction

WE HAD MANY SAINT DAYS . . . ONE TIME WE RODE FROM THE ALAMO in an oxcart to the [San Fernando] Cathedral to see the *Pastores*. It was very grand to ride and to see this blessed Shepherd Play. The altar to the Christ Child was bright with many candles. All over the plaza shone candles—the houses were all covered with lights—in remembrance of the "Light of the World."
    —Enrique Esparza, nineteenth-century San Antonian

The public rituals and fiestas at San Fernando strengthen us in our identity by allowing us to pridefully celebrate our culture and faith.
    —Dr. Frank Paredes, Jr., contemporary San Antonian

Foundational faith expressions are those religious traditions which the majority of a people celebrate voluntarily, transmit from generation to generation, and persist in celebrating with the clergy, without them, or even in spite of them. The foundational faith expressions of a people are a ritual, symbolic response to their history and contemporary situation. These expressions embody the deepest identity of the people, their collective soul. They are the people's means of encountering the God who accompanies them during times of mourning and joy, tears and laughter, rejection and welcome, hope and despair, death and life.

3

Mexican-American foundational faith expressions function as a response to their history of double conquest and their continuing struggle with assimilatory pressures, rejection, and prejudice. As a people, Mexican Americans have endured the Spanish conquest of their indigenous ancestors and the subsequent United States conquest of what is now the southwest. The influence of United States colonization continues in the pressures put on Mexican Americans to assimilate, to abandon the Mexican way for the American way. In this respect the treatment of Mexican Americans is similar to other cultural groups in the United States. The American "melting pot" has consistently exerted pressure to melt down a people's language and culture as part of the process by which they are initiated into this society. With Hispanics and other groups (most notably African Americans) from outside of Europe there is frequently a critical difference, however: skin color. While white European immigrants could blend into mainstream American society once they knew the language and culture, the ethnic origin of most Hispanics remains readily apparent. Often subtle (and not so subtle) racist treatment is the result.

The two essays in this section present the foundational faith expressions of Mexican Americans. They also examine how these expressions are a communal ritual response to their historical experience and contemporary context, the treasured ways in which the people encounter the God who accompanies them in their history and everyday lives.

1

Living Faith:
Resistance and Survival

Virgilio P. Elizondo

THE DEEPLY RELIGIOUS CHARACTER OF THE MEXICAN-AMERICAN PEOPLE
was brought into the orbit of Christianity with the coming of the
first Christian missioners in the 1500s. They embedded the te-
nets of the faith in songs, dramatizations, personal devotions,
pictures, ceremonies, and *dichos* ("sayings," "proverbs") that
were easily learned by the people. Profound theological meaning was transmitted through forms that were readily grasped
even by children.

Christianity was not so much superimposed upon as implanted and "naturalized" *in* the Mexican-American way of life.
The ensemble of the yearly celebrations of the people is equally
the *living Christian creed* of the Mexican-American ecclesial community. It does not so much *recite* the creed in an abstract way as
live it out, celebrate it, and transmit it in real life and in life-filled
celebrations. Our confession of faith is lived out in the language,
songs, gestures, dramatizations, and symbols of the people. It is
our Christian tradition. It is our creed as received, interiorized,
and expressed collectively by our faith community.

The creedal expressions of the people are sociological and
theological symbols. They are the ultimate expression of the
social level and the starting points of the theological. They en-
case in a tangible capsule the deepest truths, the mysteries, of
Christian revelation. They should be neither ignored nor taken
for granted, neither phased out nor idolized.

SYMBOLS OF ULTIMATE IDENTITY
AND BELONGING

Ash Wednesday

To anyone who knows anything about the religious practices of the Mexican-American people, it is obvious that one of the most sacred rites of the year is the reception of ashes on Ash Wednesday. For the masses of the people, this has little to do with the beginning of Lent. Lent as a season of self-sacrifice is not really of special interest to the people; the entire year is a time of suffering and abnegation.

On Ash Wednesday Mexican Americans renew their cultic communion with mother earth. For them the earth has always been sacred and they retain a fundamental identity with it. The earth supports and regenerates life; it *is* life. Living things—plants, animals, humans—come from the earth and fade back into it when they die. And the earth brings forth new life.

Foreigners may come and take away the earth from them, but they cannot take them away from the earth: the people is the living earth, the living earth is the people. When distant from their land they dream about it, sing about it. They pray that when they die they will be returned to *their* earth, there to be buried.

Their portion of the world's surface is their fundamental rooting in life, their core identity. Their ancestors came from it and returned to it. It has given them life, nourishment, shelter, clothing, a way of life, physical and psychological characteristics, the elements of their religious expressions. They live in gratitude, love, and communion with mother earth. It is God's great gift to them and the best image they know of God's creativity.

Through conquest and exploitation much of their land has been taken away from them. The sacred land—the primordial sacrament of God's continuing creation and goodness—has been divided into private fiefdoms and commercialized. Fences and political boundaries have been set up to keep them from their own land. For them this is the capital sin of *simony*—trafficking in things divine.

To deprive a people of its own land is like depriving children of their mother. Mexican Americans sense that the earth belongs to them and they to it—like mother and child. On Ash Wednesday they celebrate their personal and collective communion with their earthly basis of belonging and identity.

The rite of ashes becomes all the more significant in this era when Mexican Americans are living as captives in their own land. They are called "foreigners" and are treated as illegal intruders by another society that imposed itself on them by violence, power plays, and even religion. In their own land, their ways and their religious expressions are despised and looked down on as backward and primitive.

Their children become embarrassed about their identity because the schools and churches of the invaders tell them that the ways of white, western civilization are best. Culturally speaking, Anglo-American society is kidnapping the children of the Mexican Americans, taking them out of their own households, their own *familias*, their own *barrios*, their own land.

The rite of ashes affirms and dares to celebrate the core Mexican-American belongingness and suffering. The ashes are a sign of a suffering and death that will not be useless: even if individual persons are wiped out, the people will continue. The ashes of the present fertilize the seeds of the future.

Ash Wednesday is a day of sorrow *and* joy. The ashes are an exterior manifestation of the innermost attitude of the collective soul of the people: suffering but not despair, acceptance but not fatalism, *aguante* ("endurance") but not passive resignation, joy but not frivolity. And hope beyond immediate expectations.

Posada

One of the most popular ritual celebrations of the Mexican-American people, often organized by the *abuelitos* (the "elders," who are the carriers *par excellence* of tradition), is the *posada* ("hospitality" or "shelter" reenactment). The *posada* is a kind of Advent novena that combines prayer, songs, and games. It is the reenactment of the journey of Joseph and Mary from Nazareth to Bethlehem.

Before the procession through the *barrio*, there is an opening hymn that sets the theme of the *posada* novena, reminding the people of the meaning of what is about to take place. One group of persons then walks from house to house carrying statues of

Joseph, Mary, and the donkey. Inside each house there is a small group representing the Judeans who reject them one by one, telling them there is no room for them. Finally the small group in one of the houses invites the shelterless couple in and there is great joy in the place that welcomes them.

The apparently artless prayer-ritual text and celebration were in fact very carefully prepared by the early missioners to Mexico, concerned as they were that the essence of the gospel message reach the masses in a simple, comprehensible, and enjoyable way. Behind the gamelike appearances of the celebration, the essence of the gospel message not only came through, but was *retained* and *transmitted* from generation to generation *by the people*. Clergy at a later date, not recognizing the religious content of the *posada*, tried to substitute a cerebral catechesis for its living catechesis.

The introductory prayer-song is as follows. The words in bold type have a special significance; this will be explained at the end of the text:

Una bella pastorcita
caminaba por el frío,
y como bella rosita
va cubierta de rocío.

A beautiful shepherdess
was walking in the cold,
and, like a beautiful rose,
she was covered with dew.

Caminando va José,
caminando va María.
Caminan para Belén
más de noche que de día.

Joseph was **walking,**
Mary was **walking.**
They **walked** toward Bethlehem
more by night than by day.

Caminan de tienda en tienda,
no hay lugar en el mesón.
Todos les cierran la puerta
y también el corazón.

They **walked** from tent to tent;
there was no room in the inn.
Everyone closed their door to them,
and their hearts as well.

Humildes **peregrinos,**
Jesús, María, y José,
mi alma os doy, con ella
mi corazón también.

Humble **pilgrims,**
Jesus, Mary, and Joseph,
I give you my soul, and with it
my heart as well.

La Estrella María

Mary the Star

¿Quién es esa estrella
que a los hombres guía?
¡La Reina del Cielo,
la Virgen María!

Who is that star
that guides everyone?
The Queen of Heaven,
the Virgin Mary!

Vamos **caminando**	We are **walking**
siguiendo la huella	**following the footprints;**
todos preguntando	all are asking
quien es esa estrella.	who is that star.
Para redimirnos	To redeem us
de la idolatría	from idolatry
vino a este mundo	there came to this world
la Virgen María.	the Virgin Mary.
Las plantas florecen	The plants bloom
al ver su grandeza;	at the sight of her greatness;
los campos se alegran	the fields rejoice
al ver su belleza.	to see her beauty.
Que alegre camino	What a happy road
se ve en esta tierra;	is seen in this land;
todos de rodillas	all of us, kneeling,
estamos con ella.	are with her.
Ya supe quien eres,	I know now who you are,
madrecita bella,	beautiful mother,
de amor y placer	of love and joy,
reluciente estrella.	the shining star.

The emphasized words and phrases embody the theme of "following the way"—the brunt of the Christian Gospel preached to the people: *caminando, siguiendo la huella*, "we are walking, following the footprints." They are to walk as did the migrant shepherdess from Galilee, walking through the darkness (*más de noche que de día*) of rejection (*todos les cierran la puerta y también el corazón*) toward the light (*estrella*) that will redeem them from the idolatry of the ways of the world (*para redimirnos de la idolatría*).

The house-to-house procession then takes place, the Galilean couple—Joseph and Mary—seeking shelter (*posada*) and the Judean residents refusing their request. The pilgrimage song is as follows; the stanzas sung by those representing Joseph and Mary (in Roman print) are followed by the answers of the Judeans (in italics):

En nombre del cielo	
os pido posada	In the name of heaven
pues no puede andar	I ask you for lodging,
mi esposa amada.	because to keep on going
	my beloved wife is unable.

Aquí no es mesón,	*This is not an inn;*
sigan adelante,	*continue on your way;*
y no puedo abrir,	*I can't open [the door];*
no sea algun tunante.	*You may be riffraff.*
No seas inhumano,	Don't be inhuman;
Ténnos caridad,	have charity for us
que el Dios de los cielos	that the God of heaven
te lo premiará.	may repay you for it.
Ya se puedan ir	*You may go now*
y no molestar,	*and don't bother us,*
porque si me enfado	*because if I get angry*
os voy a apalear.	*I'm going to hit you.*
Venimos rendidos	We are very tired,
desde Nazaret.	coming from Nazareth.
Yo soy carpintero	I am a carpenter,
de nombre José.	Joseph by name.
No me importa el nombre,	*I don't care about your name;*
déjenme dormir,	*let me sleep;*
pues que ya les digo	*I already told you*
que no hemos de abrir.	*that we're not going to open.*

After the pilgrim group has been rejected by a number of households, one of them finally takes an interest and agrees to give them a place to stay:

Posada te pide,	Asking you for lodging,
amado casero,	kind homeowner,
por solo una noche	for only one night,
la Reina del Cielo.	is the Queen of Heaven.
Pues si es una reina	*If she is a queen*
quien lo solicita,	*who is asking,*
¿como es que de noche	*how is it that at night*
anda tan solita?	*she is walking alone?*
Mi esposa es María,	My wife is Mary,
es Reina del Cielo,	she is the Queen of Heaven,
y madre va a ser	and she is going to be mother
del Divino Verbo.	of the Divine Word.
¿Eres tu José?	*Are you Joseph?*
¿Tu esposa es María?	*Your wife is Mary?*
Entren peregrinos,	*Come in, pilgrims,*
no los conocía.	*I did not know who you were.*

Dios pague, señores,	May God reward, good persons,
vuestra caridad	your charity,
y así os colme el cielo	and may heaven fill you
de felicidad.	with happiness.
¡Dichosa la casa	*Happy the home*
que abriga este día	*that houses today*
a la Virgen pura,	*the pure Virgin,*
la hermosa María!	*the beautiful Mary!*
Entren santos peregrinos,	*Come in, holy pilgrims,*
reciban este rincón	*accept this corner,*
no de esta pobre morada	*not of this poor house,*
sino de mi corazón.	*but of my heart.*
Esta noche es de alegría,	*This is a night of happiness,*
de gusto y de regocijo,	*of joy and rejoicing,*
porque hospedamos aquí	*because we give hospitality here*
a la Madre de Dios Hijo.	*to the Mother of God the Son.*

The rite is centered on two experiences that bring out key themes of the gospel proclamation: the *rejection* of the poor, nameless couple from the "inferior" region of Galilee and the *joy* that comes to those who open the door of their home and heart to shelter and welcome the rejects, because they recognize them for what they truly are, God's chosen ones. It is in the poor shepherd girl from Nazareth that God now dwells. Her womb is the new temple of God's presence. God comes to make an abode among us in those whom the world rejects.

These central experiences are to be repeated in the life of Jesus. He comes from a rejected people. He experiences both the pain of rejection by those who judge themselves "superior" and the joy of being accepted and welcomed by his own.

Whereas wealthy Mexicans have turned the *posada* into an elaborate and expensive drunken brawl that has nothing to do with its original meaning, the poor and simple continue the tradition of the original *posada*. And they enter into the beginnings of the way of Jesus. Whether the church encourages them or not, these living Christian catechetical novenas continue in all *barrios* where Mexicans or Mexican Americans live. The *posada* has taken place for hundreds of years, passed on from generation to generation, without written rituals or scripts.

The *posada* is easily a *cultic* reminder and reenactment as well, for Mexican Americans who have walked, often at night and through snake-infested deserts, to the United States in the hope of finding work. What they found instead was rejection after rejection. But, like Joseph and Mary, they did not give up; they followed their star.

The *posada* is a living symbol of a living faith.

Pastorela

Another popular devotion expressing the theme of human rejection and divine election is that of the *pastorela*. The *pastorelas* are miracle plays that were started by the early missioners to allow the Indians to experience the entire drama of salvation. They started with creation, went through the fall, continued through the various struggles of the chosen people, finally coming to the birth of Christ and the adoration. They were very graphic and visual and included battles between angels and devils, the struggles of the prophets, the temptations by the devils, and finally the great conquest of the coming of Christ. These miracle plays have been handed on from generation to generation, although the scripts have never been written until very recent times. People took it upon themselves as a vow to reenact their part once a year and to prepare someone who would be able to continue when they were no longer around. *Pastorelas* were put on in the neighborhoods throughout Mexico and in many places of the southwest.

One of the things that always impressed me about the *pastorelas* was that the costumes appeared to be very shabby. I was always tempted to give the people some money so that they could buy finer materials for the costumes. Eventually I learned from them that there was a profound reason for these types of costumes. Costumes may be made only from discarded materials: in the incarnation the rejected of the world are chosen and beautified. Hence the *pastorelas* are themselves a celebration of the rejection that becomes election in the birth of Christ.

San Martín de Porres

Historians agree that the Peruvian Martín de Porres was held back for a time from full membership in the Dominican Order because of the church law barring the children of unmarried parents from entering a religious congregation. Or it may have been Martín himself, in his rugged humility, who would not ask anything for himself except the lowest place. But the masses of Latin America commonly believe that he was acted against prejudicially because of his racially mixed parentage (his father was Spanish, his mother a freed African). God worked extraordinary wonders through him; he was finally canonized by Pope John XXIII. San Martín de Porres is another example of the lesson that God chooses what humankind rejects. Church law did not allow him to be called to orders, but God called him into the communion of saints.

Diosito, Jesús, María y los Santos

Personal intimacy with God is another constant in the Mexican-American faith. It takes expression in a variety of ways. Many of the ordinary sayings of daily life are a sign of it: *Si Dios quiere* ("If God wills"); *Hágase la voluntad de Dios* ("God's will be done"); *Que Diosito te ayude* ("May God help you"); *Adios* (in the meaning: "Leave it to God"); *El hombre pone y Dios dispone* ("Man proposes, God disposes").

The terms *Diosito* and *Papacito Dios* occur frequently in ordinary conversation (from *Dios*, "God," and *Papá*, "father, dad," plus the suffix *-ito*, a diminutive implying familiarity; there are no direct equivalents in English, the closest approximations being something like "Dearest God" or "Daddy-God").

Reference to God the Father is common in poetry and song. The loving and caring presence of God is an unquestioned fact of everyday life. God is always present to the people; they live in God's presence.

In most Mexican-American homes—as in most Mexican homes—a home altar is to be found, with a crucifix, a picture or statue of Mary (usually Our Lady of Guadalupe, but sometimes another *virgencita* or several different ones together), and a picture of the Sacred Heart. There may be other statues and pictures, including one of John F. Kennedy or even the local priest. But the crucifix, the *virgencita*, and the Sacred Heart will almost always be there in a position of honor. Image-presence has always played a key role in the life and communication process of the Mexican-American people.

The Sacred Heart

It is important to know that deep in the Mexican personality *rostro y corazón* ("countenance and heart") have always been the revelation of the human personality in action. The word "heart" continues to be used in Mexican and Mexican-American Spanish to refer to persons loved. The heart is the symbol of the person. And because their knowledge or awareness of Christ is not so much through the medium of messianic titles or of doctrine, but through their personal and intimate friendship with Jesus of Nazareth, it is the heart that best expresses it.

The Sacred Heart is the symbol that best images the full reality of Jesus to the Mexican American: unlimited, unconditioned love. They want to relate to a living Christ who has an understanding face and a compassionate heart. Mexican Americans are not satisfied with *reading* the truth; they want to *see* the truth. And it is in the image of the Sacred Heart that they "see" the truth of Jesus and the Father fully revealed.

Eucharistic Presence

The presence of Christ in the eucharist—Corpus Christi processions, the night watch on Holy Thursday, the presence in the tabernacle—has been another sensible and communitarian experience of the closeness of the Lord to the Mexican-American people. The Cursillo movement was especially successful in promoting a keen sense of the real presence of Christ as Lord and brother. I have often observed Mexican Americans kneeling before the Blessed Sacrament, discussing their problems and hopes—and I find it very natural to do so myself.

Christ the King

As the masses of the Mexican people became more and more dissatisfied with the abuses heaped on them by successive governments, they became convinced that Christ alone could be trusted as ruler and king. In contrast to the European experience, where devotion to Christ the King seems to have been promoted as a final defense of monarchy, in Mexico it became the symbol of ultimate defiance to a tyrannical government. If politicians could not be trusted, then in the name of the true king, Christ the Lord, they must be overthrown.

In the late 1920s the Cristero movement (from *Cristo Rey*) reproached the Mexican government for its restrictive measures like the ban on all religious services in the nation's Catholic churches. The solemnities of Christ the King were celebrated throughout the nation despite the government's stand. In Mexico City two hundred thousand people paraded through the streets shouting *"¡Viva Cristo Rey, Viva la Virgen Morena, Viva el Papa, Viva el arzobispo, Viva el clero mexicano!"* ("Long live Christ the King . . . the Dark Virgin . . . the pope . . . the archbishop . . . the Mexican clergy!").

Inasmuch as the Mexican and Mexican-American peoples have never lived under a government that was truly for the people and by the people, the theme of the kingdom of *Cristo nuestro Rey* continues to be very real in their lives. It is not something separate from the theme of rejection and acceptance, but a development and implementation of it. In the theme of the kingdom some of the nuclear aspects of the way of Jesus are brought out more explicitly: intimacy with the Father is blended with intimacy with Jesus, with the saints, with one another. The fundamental equality and dignity of each person is affirmed as the only true basis of human society and governance.

SYMBOLS OF STRUGGLE, SUFFERING, AND DEATH

It should not be surprising that devotion to the crucified Lord—scourged, bleeding, agonizing—is one of the deepest traits of the Mexican-American faith. *Cruz* ("cross") is a not uncommon name given to their children.

El Viernes Santo (Good Friday) is the Mexican-American celebration *par excellence*. The commemoration of the Lord's crucifixion is the celebration of their life—a life of suffering. Their daily life is assumed in his death and therein defies the anomalies of life.

Why is the "scandal" of the cross as necessary for salvation today as it was for Jesus? Because the cross continues to reveal the impurity of the pure and the purity of the impure, the innocence of criminals and the crimes of the innocent, the righteousness of sinners and the sin of the righteous, the wisdom of the foolish and the foolishness of the wise.

Some persons working with Mexican Americans have thought it would be better to shift the emphasis from the cross to the resurrection. I would agree *if* the situation were changing in such a way that we could say that resurrection was indeed becoming a meaningful symbol. But this is not yet the case. I agree with Jesuit theologian Jon Sobrino that the point is not to do away with the people's celebration of the cross, but to help them appreciate better Jesus' active march toward the cross, so they will see that it was more than passive suffering on the cross. In the long run, of course, this march would be meaningless without the resurrection; human suffering, as imaged in the crucifixion, would be devoid of sense. Jesus did not *start* with the cross, nor was it the only element in his salvific ministry.

The drama of Good Friday is not just celebrated ritually in the churches but lived out by the Mexican-American people. It begins on Holy Thursday with the agony in the garden. On Good Friday the Way of the Cross is reenacted by the people. The crucifixion and the *siete palabras* (the seven last words of Jesus from the cross) follow. Finally, in the evening, there is the *pésame a la Virgen* ("condolences to the Virgin"). Never was the distance between the "official" church and the church of the people more evident to me than on Good Friday in Mexico City where there might be as few as a hundred people in a *barrio* church for the official services and as many as sixty thousand outside the building, taking part in a living Way of the Cross.

To "academic" theologians and liturgists this may seem a folkloric, nostalgic, emotional, childish expression of religion; they would not call it *real* liturgy. But for a people for whom sudden arrest, speedy trial, trumped-up charges, circumstantial evidence, quick verdict, and immediate sentencing are a way of life—as is true for the millions of poor and oppressed throughout Latin America and in the United States—this ritual reenactment of the way of Jesus is the *supreme* liturgy. It is the celebration of their creed. It is not academic theorization; it is life.

Mary's role in the crucifixion of her Son is relived by millions of women in Latin America—grandmothers, mothers, wives, girlfriends. They stand by silently as injustice, violence, is done to their loved ones. They are silent not because they are afraid or because they agree with the civil authorities, but because they do not even understand the language. They are silent because they know, through their collective experience with other women who have gone through similar experiences, that they are powerless against the authorities: *"Pues no sé, Padrecito, se lo llevaron las autoridades . . . no hay nada que se pueda hacer"* ("I don't know, the authorities took him away, Padre . . . there's nothing to be done"). They are silent not only because they do not have the money to hire a lawyer, but because they probably do not even know about the existence of lawyers. They are silent because if they said something, reprisals might be taken against other members of the family.

Thousands of persons watch their loved ones be taken away, accused of some crime, condemned, and sentenced by the "justice of the powerful"—and all they can do is stand silently by them to the very end. I have myself met many such men and women in the jails of San Antonio. They do not even know why they are there. Some just happened to be standing by when a crime was committed. Their family has no money for bail. They do not know their way around. All they could do was pray and patiently wait and hope that something would be worked out.

The final Good Friday reenactment is the burial service. Some ridicule this popular rite of the burial of Jesus and attribute its popularity to the "morbid" inclinations of the Mexican Americans—"always preoccupied with death." But when it is realized that even in death this people is rejected, the quiet, almost clandestine, burial of Jesus takes on a deeper significance for them. Segregated cemeteries are still a commonplace, even if not segregated as in the past—along skin-color lines.

The Mexican-American people have a very special devotion to *nuestro Diosito en la cruz*. Good Friday is *nuestra fiesta*, the cultic celebration of *nuestra existencia*. It is not an "other-worldly" make believe; it is a celebration of *nuestra vida*.

SYMBOLS OF NEW CREATION

The happiness and joy of the Mexican and Mexican-American peoples is immediately obvious to outsiders. The tragedies of their history have not obliterated laughter and joy, warm friendship and the capacity to love.

The Mexican-American propensity for celebration is something that others find extremely difficult to understand. Outsiders may enjoy but they cannot enter fully into the spirit of a fiesta or imitate one on their own. But anyone who has attended a Mexican-American fiesta knows that celebration has taken place. There is spontaneity and ritual, joy and sorrow, music and silence.

Fiesta is the mystical celebration of a complex identity, the mystical affirmation that life is a gift and is worth living. In the fiesta the fatalistic/pessimistic realism and the adventuresome/optimistic idealism of the Mexican heritage are blended into the one celebration of the mystery of life—a series of apparent contradictions never fully comprehended but assumed, transcended, celebrated. In the fiesta the Mexican American rises above the quest for the logical meaning of life and celebrates the very contradictions that are the essence of the mystery of human life.

The Fiesta of Our Lady of Guadalupe

Two Mexican-American celebrations stand out as the most universal: the collective celebration of the fiesta of Our Lady of Guadalupe and the family celebration of the baptism of an infant. The two celebrations are interrelated in the identification of the people as *la raza*, as a cultural and religious entity.

Because of the historical process that has been taking place over the past four hundred years and continues today, the cultural elements in the Mexican-American identity cannot be fully separated from the religious elements. The Gospel and the culture are not fully identified with each other, but they cannot be fully separated. The Gospel has been transforming the culture and the culture has been reactualizing the Gospel through its own vital expressions.

If Ash Wednesday stresses the earthly belonging and present suffering of the people and Good Friday marks their collective struggles and death, the feast of Our Lady of Guadalupe shouts out with joy the proclamation that a new dawn is breaking: the collective resurrection of a new people. Out of their own earth—Tepeyac—and in continuity with the life of their ancestors, a new mother emerges, pregnant with new life. She is not a goddess but the new woman from whom the new humanity will be born, *la raza cósmica de las Américas*. She is herself the prototype of the new creation. She is *la Mestiza*. She combines opposing forces so that in a creative way new life, not destruction, will emerge. On 12 December is celebrated the beginning of the new human-divine adventure.

It is important to remember that *flowers* were the sign that *la Morenita* gave to prove that she was God's messenger. In ancient and contemporary Mexican culture flowers are a sign of new existence. From the seeds that fall to earth, seeds which are watered by the heavenly dew and fertilized by the ashes and remains of previous life, new life comes forth.

The resurrection of Christ was the beginning of the new Christian people, uniting and transcending natural peoples without destroying them. Something similar happened at Guadalupe. Mexicans discovered that they were a new people, reborn.

On the feast of Our Lady of Guadalupe the people come together early in the morning to celebrate the irruption of new life—the dawn of a new humanity. This is the Easter sunrise service of the people. Before the first rays of the sun, they come together to sing *Las Mañanitas* which is our proclamation of new life. It is the roses of Tepeyac that take the place of the Easter lilies of Western Christianity.

Guadalupe was also a *pentecost* event: it opened the way to true dialogue between Europeans and Mexican Indians. It was a symbol of unity over and above their many and serious diversities. It marked the beginning of the fusion of two mother cultures—the Spanish and the Mexican Indian—which in turn gave birth to a *mestizo* culture. *La Morenita* became the "mother of all the inhabitants of this land." Individuals who found themselves divided and segregated on the basis of human barriers—external differences—discovered that they were united in something far more important than what divided them: a common mother. Mexico is a very divided nation and there is no doubt to anyone working with Mexican Americans in the United States that they constitute a very divided people. But there is likewise a very strong unity and spirit of *familia* among this divided people.

It has been held that the symbolism of Guadalupe works to canonize and maintain *divisions* among the Mexican-American people. I have to admit that in some ways this does happen. But there is another function to the symbol: it gives a basis for a much deeper unity than does any class-struggle model. The power of Guadalupe is that it signals a common motherhood for all the inhabitants of the land. As new models of society are proposed and begin to be worked out, when they persuade some individuals to think of themselves as inferior and others as superior, the conviction of a fellowship of equals under a common mother cannot find realization. Conversely, when individuals have become aware of their basic equality and see that it is not embodied in their society, they will work and struggle to bring about new lifestyles more reflective of the fundamental reality that all are children of the same mother.

La Morenita is found not only in the basilica in Mexico City but in numberless shrines throughout the Americas, in the homes of millions of persons, on medals around the necks of men, women, and children, tattooed on the arms and chests of men, sung about in pop songs, painted on the walls of barrios from California to Texas. Our Lady did not appear once and for all in 1531: she continues to appear wherever Mexican Americans find themselves in the world today.

Our Lady did not simply tell the Indians to build her a temple. She sent them to the bishop—the representative of the institutional church. It was to be the people—the whole church—that would build the new temple of compassion. The message was twofold: the Indians, in the person of Juan Diego, were to go to the bishop (the church), and the church (in the person of the bishop) was to build a temple among the people.

In her telling the people through Juan Diego "Go to the bishop . . . ," we can glimpse a reflection of her telling the waiters at Cana "Do whatever he tells you . . ." (Jn 2:5). And what she tells the church is to "build a temple . . . of compassion"—a way of life in which compassion, mercy, and love will reign. In other words, her command, understood in this broader sense, was: "Incarnate the Gospel among this people so that Christ will not come as a stranger but as one of them."

Mary's command to the Mexican church in 1531 was echoed by the Synod of Bishops in 1977 when it recognized and stressed the obligation on the part of the church to inculturate the Gospel among the peoples of diverse cultures in order for it to be understood and lived by them. Without this inculturation—mestizaje—of the Gospel into the natural substratum of a people's life, the Gospel will never truly be implanted and a truly local church will never emerge.

Baptism

In the seven years that followed the apparition of Guadalupe in 1531, some eight million persons came to the church asking for baptism. They came in large groups and from great distances, reminiscent of the baptisms following the sermons of St. Peter in the infant church.

Baptism has always played a very special role in the lives of the Mexican and Mexican-American peoples. The baptized infant enters into the collective identity and life of the family, the group, and the people. Baptism has never been thought of as simply the entry of another individual into the institutional church. In baptism the child is accepted and welcomed (recall the *posada* imagery) into the life and memory of the entire family—parents, siblings, grandparents, relatives, and in-laws. The newly baptized becomes *uno de los nuestros* ("one of ours"). What the people celebrate collectively on the feast of Guadalupe, they celebrate individually in the baptism of a child: rebirth and the promise of new life.

2

Popular Religion as Support of Identity

Virgilio P. Elizondo

THE MEXICAN AMERICAN IS ONE WHO THROUGH BIRTH OR ACQUIRED nationality is *a citizen of the United States while maintaining a deep Mexican heritage.* Today there are approximately 14,300,000 Mexican Americans in the United States, and the number continues to increase daily. It is a highly complex socio-cultural group that is quite at home in the United States without ever fully assimilating the United States way of life. It is neither fully North American nor fully Latin American. It lived in its present day geographical setting long before the United States migrated west and took over the Mexican territories. One of the key factors in the identity, cohesiveness, and continuity of the group is the persistence of its religious symbolism which we will explore briefly in this presentation.

FUNCTION OF RELIGIOUS SYMBOLS

The popular expressions of the faith *function in totally different ways for various peoples depending on their history and socio-cultural status.* For the dominant culture, the popular expressions of the faith will serve to legitimize their way of life as God's true way for humanity. They will tranquilize the moral conscience and blind people from seeing the injustices which exist in daily life. For a colonized/oppressed/dominated group, they are the ultimate resistance to the attempts of the dominant culture to destroy them as a distinct group either through annihilation or through absorption and total assimilation. They will maintain alive the sense of injustice to which the people are subjected in their daily lives.

By popular expressions of the faith I do not refer to the private or individual devotions of a few people but to the *ensemble of beliefs, rituals, ceremonies, devotions, and prayers which are commonly practiced by the people at large*. It is my contention, which is beyond the scope of this paper to develop but which will be its point of departure, that those expressions of the faith which are celebrated voluntarily by the majority of the people, transmitted from generation to generation by the people themselves and which go on with the church, without it or even in spite of it, express the *deepest identity of the people*. They are the ultimate foundation of the people's innermost being and the common expression of the collective soul of the people. They are supremely meaningful for the people who celebrate them and meaningless to the outsider. To the people whose very life-source they are, no explanation is necessary, but to the casual or scientific spectator no explanation will ever express or communicate their true and full meaning. Without them there might be associations of individuals bound together by common interest (e.g., the corporation, the State, etc.), but there will never be the experience of being a people.

It is within the context of the tradition of the group that one experiences both a sense of *selfhood* and a sense of *belonging*. Furthermore, it is within the tradition that one remains in contact both with one's beginnings through the genealogies and the stories of origins and with one's ultimate end. We are born into them and within them we discover our full and ultimate being. I might enjoy and admire other traditions very much, but I will never be fully at home within them. No matter how much I get into them, I will always have a sense of being other.

From the very beginning, Christianity presented a very unique way of universalizing peoples without destroying their localized identity. People would neither have to disappear through assimilation nor be segregated as inferior. The Christian message interwove with the local religious traditions so as to give the people a deeper sense of local identity (a sense of rootedness) while at the same time breaking down the psycho-sociological barriers that kept nationalities separate and apart from each other so as to allow for a truly universal fellowship (a sense of universality). In other words, it *affirmed rootedness while destroying ghettoishness*. Christianity changed peoples and cultures not by destroying them, but by reinterpreting their core rituals and myths through the foundational ritual and myth of Christianity. Thus, now a Jew could still be a faithful Jew and yet belong fully to the new universal fellowship and equally a Greek or a Roman could still be fully Greek or Roman and equally belong to the new universal group.

RELIGIOUS TRADITIONS OF THE AMERICAS

The beginning of the Americas introduces two *radically distinct image/myth representations* of the Christian tradition. The United States *was born as a secular enterprise* with a deep sense of religious mission. The native religions were eliminated and totally supplanted by a new type of religion: Puritan moralism, Presbyterian righteousness, and Methodist social consciousness coupled with deism and the spirit of rugged individualism to provide a sound basis for the new nationalism which would function as the core religion of the land. It was *quite different in Latin America* where the religion of the old world clashed with those of the new, and in their efforts to uproot the native religions, Iberian Catholics found themselves totally assumed into them. Iberian Catholicism with its emphasis on clerical rituals and the divinely established monarchical nature of all society conquered physically but itself *was absorbed by the pre-Colombian spiritualism* with its emphasis on the harmonious unity of opposing tensions: male and female, suffering and happiness, self-annihilation and transcendence, individual and group, sacred and profane. In the secular-based culture of the United States, it is the one who succeeds materially who appears to be the upright and righteous person—the good and saintly. In the pre-Colombian/Iberian-Catholic *mestizo*-based culture of Mexico, it is the one who can endure all the opposing tensions of life and not lose his or her interior harmony who appears to be the upright and righteous one.

With the great western expansion of the United States in the 1800s, *fifty percent of northern Mexico was conquered* and taken over by the United States. The Mexicans living in that vast region spanning a territory of over 3500 kilometers from California to Texas suddenly became aliens in their own land . . . foreigners who never left home. Their entire way of life was despised. The Mexican *mestizo* was abhorred as a mongrel who was good only for cheap labor. Efforts were instituted to *suppress everything Mexican: customs, language and Mexican Catholicism*. The fair-skinned, blond Mexicans who remained had the choice of assimilating totally to the white, Anglo-Saxon Protestant culture of the United States or being ostracized as an inferior human being. The dark-skinned had no choice! They were marked as an inferior race destined to be the servants of the white master race.

Today, social unrest and dire poverty force many people from Mexico to move to the former Mexican territories which politically are part of the United States. Newcomers are harassed by the immigration services of the United States as illegal intruders—a curious irony since it was the United States which originally entered this region illegally and stole it from Mexico. Yet the descendants of the original settlers of this region plus those who have immigrated continue to feel at home, to resist efforts of destruction through assimilation and to celebrate their legitimacy as a people.

MEXICAN AMERICAN RELIGIOUS SYMBOLS

The Mexican Americans living in that vast borderland between the United States and Mexico have *not only survived* as a unique people but *have even maintained good mental health* in spite of the countless insults and put-downs suffered throughout their history and even in the present moment of time.[1] Anyone who has suffered such a long history of segregation, degradation, and exploitation should be a mental wreck.[2] Yet, despite their ongoing suffering, not only are the numbers increasing, but in general they are prospering, joyful, and healthy thanks to the profound faith of the people as lived and expressed through the common religious practices of the group. I could explore many of them,[3] but I will limit myself to what I consider to be the *three sets of related core expressions* which mark the ultimate ground, the perimeters, and the final aspirations of the Mexican-American people: *Guadalupe/Baptism; dust/water; crucifixion/the "dead" ones.*

They are the symbols in which the apparently destructive forces of life are assumed, transcended, and united. In them we experience the ultimate meaning and destiny of our life pilgrimage.

There is no greater and more persistent symbol of Mexican and Mexican-American identity than devotion to Our Lady of Guadalupe. Thousands visit her home at Tepeyac each day and she keeps reappearing daily throughout the Americas in the spontaneous prayers and artistic expressions of the people. In her the people experience acceptance, dignity, love, and protection . . . they dare to affirm life even when all others deny them life. Since her apparition she has been the flag of all the great movements of independence, betterment, and liberty.

Were it not for Our Lady of Guadalupe[4] there would be no Mexican or Mexican-American people today. The great Mexican nations had been defeated by the Spanish invasion which came to a violent and bloody climax in 1521. The native peoples who had not been killed no longer wanted to live. Everything of value to them, including their gods, had been destroyed. Nothing was worth living for. With this colossal catastrophe their entire past became irrelevant. New diseases appeared and, together with the trauma of the collective death-wish of the people, the native population decreased enormously.

It was *in the brown Virgin of Guadalupe that Mexicanity was born* and through her that the people have survived and developed. At the very moment when the pre-Colombian world had come to a drastic end, a totally unsuspected irruption took place in 1531 when, in the ancient site of the goddess Tonantzin, a *mestiza* woman appeared to announce a new era for "all the inhabitants of this land." Guadalupe provides the spark that will allow the people to arise out of the realm of death like the rising phoenix arising out of the ashes of the past—not just a return to the past but the emergence of a spectacular newness.[5] In sharp contrast to the total rupture with the past which was initiated by the conquest-evangelization enterprise, Guadalupe provided the necessary *sense of continuity* which is basic to human existence. Since the apparition took place at Tepeyac, the long-venerated site of the goddess Tonantzin, it put people in direct contact with their ancient past and in communion with their own foundational mythology. It validated their ancestry while initiating them into something new. The missioners had said their ancestors had been wrong and that the diabolical past had to be totally eradicated. But the lady who introduced herself as the mother of the true God was now appearing among them and asking that a *temple* be built on this sacred site. Out of their own past and in close continuity with it, something truly sacred was now emerging.

Furthermore, she was giving meaning to the present moment in several ways for she was promising them love, defense, and protection. At a time when the people had experienced the abandonment of their gods, the mother of the true God was now offering them her personal intervention. At a time when new racial and ethnic divisions were emerging, she was offering the basis of a new unity as the mother of all the inhabitants of the land. At a time when the natives were being instructed and told what to do by the Spaniards, she chose a low class Indian to be her trusted messenger who was to instruct the Spaniards through the person of the bishop and tell them what to do.

Finally, she initiated and proclaimed the new era which was now beginning. Over her womb is the Aztec glyph for the center of the universe. Thus she carries the force that will gradually build up the civilization which will be neither a simple restoration of the past nor simply New Spain, but the beginning of something new. The sign of flowers, which she provided as a sign of her authenticity, was for the Indian world the sign which guaranteed that the new life would truly flourish.

Thus in Guadalupe the *ancient beginnings connect with the present moment and point to what is yet to come!* The broken pieces of their ancient numinous world are now re-pieced in a totally new way. Out of the chaos a new world of ultimate meaning is now emerging. The phoenix had truly come forth not just as a powerful new life, but also as the *numinosum* which would allow them to once again experience the awe and reverence of the sacred—not a sacred which was foreign and opposed to them, but one which ultimately legitimized them in their innermost being—both collectively as a people and individually as persons.

The second great religious expression is the baptism of infants. Our Lady of Guadalupe had sent the Indian Juan Diego to the church. The Indian world immediately started to go to church and ask for baptism. Yet, they were no longer being uprooted totally from their ancient ways in order to enter the church. They were entering as they were—with their customs, their rituals, their songs, their dances, and their pilgrimages. The old Franciscan missioners feared this greatly. Many thought it was a devil's trick to subvert their missionary efforts. But the people kept on coming. They were truly building the new temple the Lady had requested: the living temple of Mexican Christians. It is through baptism that every newborn Mexican enters personally into the temple requested by the Lady. Through baptism the child becomes part of the continuum and is guaranteed life in spite of the social forces against life. The community claims the child as its very own and with pride presents it to the entire people. In the group the child will receive great affirmation and tenderness. This will give the child a profound sense of existential security. He/she will be able to affirm selfhood despite the put-downs and insults of society: they will dare to be who they are—and they will be who they are with a great sense of pride!

The ashes of the beginning of Lent are a curious and mysterious religious expression of the Mexican tradition which finds its full socio-religious meaning when coupled with the holy water blessed during the Easter Vigil. For people who have been forced to become foreigners in their own land, who have been driven from their properties, and who have been pushed around by the powerful in the way the mighty wind blows the dust around, ashes, as a moment of the continuum of the pilgrimage of life, become most powerful. They mark the radical acceptance of the moment—actually there is no choice. But this is not the end, for the people do not only come for ashes. Throughout the year they come for *holy water* to sprinkle upon themselves, their children, their homes . . . everything. They are very aware that our entire world yearns and travails in pain awaiting to be redeemed—a redemption which in Christ has indeed begun but whose rehabilitating effects are yet to take effect in our world of present-day injustices. The sprinkling with the waters of the Easter vigil is a constant call for the *regeneration of all creation*. The dust which is sprinkled with the water will be turned into fertile earth and produce in great abundance. As in the reception of ashes there is an acceptance, in the sprinkling of holy water there is an unquestioned affirmation: the ashes will again become earth; the dust-people will become the fertile earth and the earth will once again be ours. The *dust-water binomial* symbolizes the great suffering of an uprooted people who refuse to give in to despair but live in the unquestioned hope of the new life that is sure to come.

The final set of religious celebrations that express the core identity of the Mexican-American people is the crucifixion which is celebrated on Good Friday and the dead whose day is celebrated on 2 November. For a people who have consistently been subjected to injustice, cruelty, and early death, the image of the crucified is the supreme symbol of life despite the multiple daily threats of death. If there was something good and redemptive in the unjust condemnation and crucifixion of the God-man, then, as senseless and useless as our suffering appears to be, there must be something of ultimate goodness and transcendent value in it. We don't understand it, but in Jesus the God-man who suffered for our salvation, we affirm it and in this very affirmation receive the power to endure it without it destroying us. *Even if we are killed, we cannot be destroyed.* This is the curious irony of our celebrations of the dead: they appear to be dead, but they are not really dead! For they live not only in God but in our hearts and in our memory. Those whom the world thinks are dead . . . those who have been killed by society . . . defy death and are alive in us. In our celebrations of memory, their presence is keenly experienced. Thus what is celebrated as the day of the dead is in effect the celebration of life—a life which not even death can destroy. Society might take our lands away, marginate us, and even kill us, but it cannot destroy us. For we live on in the generations to come and in them we continue to be alive.

CONCLUSION

The *conquest of ancient Mexico by Spain in 1521* and then the *conquest of northern Mexico by the United States in the 1840s* forced the native population and their succeeding generations into a split and meaningless existence. It was a mortal collective catastrophe of gigantic death-bearing consequences. Yet the people have survived as a people through the *emergence of new religious symbols* and the reinterpretation of old ones which have connected the past with the present and projected into the future. The core religious expressions as celebrated and transmitted by the people are the unifying symbols in which the opposing forces of life are brought together into a harmonious tension so as to give the people who participate in them the experience of *wholeness*. In them and through them, opposites are brought together and push towards a resolution and the people who celebrate them experience an overcoming of the split. Where formerly there was opposition, now there is reconciliation and even greater yet, synthesis. This is precisely what gives joy and meaning to life, indeed makes life possible in any meaningful sense regardless of the situation. It is in the celebration of these festivals of being and memory that the people live on as a people.

Notes

1. Rodolfo Acuña, *Occupied America: A History of Chicanos* (New York: Harper & Row, 1981).

2. Roberto Jimenez, "Social Changes/Emotional Health," *Medical Gazette of South Texas* 7 (20 June 1985).

3. For a further discussion of other religious symbols, consult my previous works: *Christianity and Culture* (San Antonio: Mexican American Cultural Center Press, 1975); *La Morenita: Evangelizer of the Americas* (San Antonio: Mexican American Cultural Center Press, 1980); *Galilean Journey: The Mexican-American Promise* (Maryknoll, N.Y.: Orbis, 1983).

4. For other aspects of Guadalupe, consult my: "Our Lady of Guadalupe as a Cultural Symbol: 'The Power of the Powerless'" in *Liturgy and Cultural Religious Traditions*, ed. Herman Schmidt and David Power (New York: Seabury, 1977) 25-33; "Mary and the Poor: A Model of Evangelizing Ecumenism," in *Mary in the Churches*, ed. Hans Küng and Jürgen Moltmann (New York: Seabury, 1983) 59-65. The former article is the third essay in this collection.

5. J. Ruffie, *De la biologie à la culture* (Paris, 1976) 247-252.

PART TWO

Guadalupe and the
Two Conquests

Introduction

On the 12th of December, the feast of Our Lady of Guadalupe, the patroness of Mexico, and of all the Spanish colonies, the inhabitants of San Antonio, who, in more prosperous times, solemnized this day with great rejoicings, felt their ancient zeal for the veneration of Mary revived.
—Jean Marie Odin, first bishop of Texas, 1842

Were it not for Our Lady of Guadalupe there would be no Mexican or Mexican-American people today.
—Virgilio P. Elizondo

A key element in the history of Mexican Americans is that they have been twice colonized. The first conquest was the Spanish conquest of the indigenous peoples of what is now Mexico and the southwest United States. Beginning with the arrival of Hernán Cortés on 22 April 1519, this conquest subjugated the native peoples and imposed Spanish rule and culture on them. The worst aspect of this conquest was not the military defeat, nor the economic exploitation, nor even the rape and enslavement of the people, but the attempt to destroy their world view, rituals, and symbols—the very means by which a group sustains meaning in its existence.

The second conquest was that of the southwest, initiated in the war between Texas and Mexico (1836) and later completed in

35

the Mexican-American War (1846-1848). This latter war between the United States and Mexico resulted from the Manifest Destiny policy that characterized the expansionist program of the United States. The results of this conquest were as catastrophic as the first; from California to Texas Mexican residents suddenly became aliens in their own land, foreigners who never left home. Their entire way of life was despised and the conquerors instituted efforts to suppress everything Mexican: their customs, their language, and even their Mexican Catholicism.

Our Lady of Guadalupe accompanied and aided the people during these times of conquest. Her appearances to Juan Diego in 1531 brought the fallen indigenous peoples back to life. Ongoing Guadalupan devotion in what is now the southwest enabled the conquered Mexican population to endure suffering, confront social upheaval with faith, and resist the diminishment of their religious and cultural heritage. The two essays in this section examine the historical role of Guadalupe, the mother of the vanquished, during the two conquests.

3

Our Lady of Guadalupe as a Cultural Symbol

Virgilio P. Elizondo

NOWADAYS WE REALIZE THAT RELIGIOUS SYMBOLS WHICH THE THEOLO-gian has labeled as "popular" religion and has looked upon as a species of pagan practice do not have to be rejected, but reinterpreted. In past decades the tendency of rational theology was to consider symbols as fantasies, to underline their ambiguity, and therefore to speak of them only in negative terms. This leads to an opposition between the religion of the people, which is not looked upon as true faith, and faith in Christ, which appears as the religion of the intellectual elite. A closer view of reality leads to a different understanding.[1] Even to the theologian, popular devotion appears ambiguous; nevertheless, it is the way the people relate to the God of Jesus. Therefore, from the pastoral as well as from the theological point of view, we have to try to answer the following question: What is the meaning of popular symbols and how do they function in relation to the Gospel? In this chapter I will try to clarify the problem by considering one of the most important living symbols of the Catholicism of the Americas: Our Lady of Guadalupe.

If Our Lady of Guadalupe had not appeared, the collective struggles of the Mexican people to find meaning in their chaotic existence would have created her. The cultural clash[2] of six-teenth-century Spain and Mexico was reconciled in the brown Lady of Tepeyac[3] in a way no other symbol can rival. In her the new *mestizo*[4] race, born of the violent encounter between Europe and indigenous America, finds its meaning, uniqueness, and unity. Guadalupe is the key to understanding the Christianity of the New World[5] and the Christian consciousness of the Mexicans and the Mexican Americans of the United States.

HISTORICAL CONTEXT OF THE APPARITION

To appreciate the profound meaning of Guadalupe it is important to know the historical setting at the time of the apparition. Suddenly an exterior force, the white men of Europe, intruded on the closely-knit and well-developed system of time-space relationships of the pre-Colombian civilizations.[6] Neither had ever heard of the other, nor had any suspicion that the other group existed. Western historiographers have studied the conquest from the justifying viewpoint of the European colonizers, but there is another aspect, that of the conquered. With the conquest, the world of the indigenous peoples of Mexico had, in effect, come to an end. The final battles in 1521 were not just a victory in warfare but the end of a civilization. At first, some tribes welcomed the Spaniards and joined them in the hope of being liberated from Aztec domination. Only after the conquest did they discover that the defeat of the Aztecs was in effect the defeat of all the natives of their land.[7] This painful Calvary of the Mexican people began when Cortés landed on Good Friday, 22 April 1519. It ended with the final battle on 13 August 1521. It was a military as well as a theological overthrow; their capital had been conquered, their women violated, their temples destroyed, and their gods defeated.

We cannot allow the cruelty of the conquest to keep us from appreciating the heroic efforts of the early missioners. Their writings indicated that it was their intention to found a new Christianity more in conformity with the Gospel, not simply a continuation of that in Europe. They had been carefully prepared by the universities of Spain. Immediate efforts were made to evangelize the native Mexicans. The life style of the missioners, austere poverty and simplicity, was in stark contrast to that of the conquistadors. Attempts were made to become one with the people and to preach the Gospel in the people's own language and through their customs and traditions.

Yet the missioners were limited by the socio-religious circumstances of their time. Dialogue was severely limited since neither side understood the other. The Spaniards judged the Mexican world from within the categories of their own Spanish world vision. Iberian communication was based on philosophical and theological abstractions and direct, precise speech. The missioners were convinced that truth in itself was sufficient to bring rational persons to conversion. They were not aware of the totally different way of communicating truth, especially divine truth, which the native Mexicans believed could only be adequately communicated through flower and song.[8] Even the best of the missioners could not penetrate the living temple of the Mexican consciousness.

This was also the time of the first *audiencia* of Guzmán which was noted for its corruption and abuses of the Indians. During this period the church was in constant conflict with the civil authorities because of these authorities' excessive avarice, corruption, and cruel treatment of the natives. The friars were good men who gradually won the love and respect of the common people. However, the religious convictions of generations would not give way easily, especially those of a people who firmly believed that the traditions of their ancestors were the way of the gods. As the friars tried to convert the wise men of the Indians by well-prepared theological exposition, the Indians discovered that the friars were in effect trying to eliminate the religion of their ancestors. The shock of human sacrifices led many of the missioners to see everything else in the native religion as diabolical, whereas the shock of the Spaniards' disregard for life by killing in war kept the Indians from seeing anything good or authentic in the conquerors' religion. This mutual scandal made communication difficult.[9] Furthermore, the painful memory of the conquest and new hardships imposed upon the Indians made listening to a "religion of love" difficult. Efforts to communicate remained at the level of words, but never seemed to penetrate to the level of the symbols of the people, which contained the inner meanings of their world vision. For the Indians these attempts at conversion by total rupture with the ways of their ancestors were a deeper form of violence than the physical conquest itself. Christianity had in some fashion been brought over, but it had not yet been implanted. The Indians and missioners heard each other's words but interpretation was at a standstill. Many heroic efforts were made, but little fruit had been produced. The missioners continued in prayer and self-sacrifice to ask for the ability to communicate the Gospel.

THE APPARITIONS AND THEIR MEANING

In 1531, ten years after the conquest, an event happened whose origins are clouded in mystery, yet its effects have been monumental and continuous. Early documentation about what happened does not exist, yet the massive effect which the appearance of Our Lady of Guadalupe had and continues to have on the Mexican people cannot be denied. The meaning of the happening has been recorded throughout the years in the collective memory of the people. Whatever happened in 1531 is not past history but continues to live, to grow in meaning, and to influence the lives of millions today.

According to the legend, as Juan Diego, a Christianized Indian of common status, was going from his home in the *barriada* near Tepeyac, he heard beautiful music. As he approached the source of the music, a lady appeared to him speaking in Nahuatl, the language of the conquered. She commanded Juan Diego to go to the palace of the archbishop of Mexico at Tlatelolco and to tell him that the Virgin Mary, "Mother of the true God through whom one lives" wanted a temple to be built at Tepeyac so that in it she "can show and give forth all my love, compassion, help, and defense to all the inhabitants of this land . . . . to hear their lamentations and remedy their miseries, pain, and sufferings." After two unsuccessful attempts to convince the bishop of the Lady's authenticity, the Virgin wrought a miracle. She sent Juan Diego to pick roses in a place where only desert plants existed. Then she arranged the roses in his cloak and sent him to the bishop with the sign he had demanded. As Juan Diego unfolded his cloak in the presence of the bishop, the roses fell to the ground and the image of the Virgin appeared on his cloak.

The Mexican people came to life again because of Guadalupe. Their response was a spontaneous explosion of pilgrimages, festivals, and conversions to the religion of the Virgin. Out of the meaningless and chaotic existence of the post-conquest years, a new meaning erupted. The immediate response of the church ranged from silence to condemnation. Early sources indicate that the missioners, at least those who were writing, were convinced that it was an invention of the Indians and an attempt to reestablish their previous religion. Yet gradually the church accepted the apparition of Guadalupe as the Virgin Mary, mother of God. In 1754 Pope Benedict XIV officially recognized the Guadalupe tradition by bringing it into the official liturgy of the church.

To understand the response of Juan Diego and the Mexican people, it is necessary to view the event not through Western categories of thought but through the system of communication of the Nahuatls at that time. What for the Spanish was an apparition for the conquered and dying Mexican nation was the rebirth of a new civilization. The details of the image conveyed a profound meaning to the Indian peoples. In reading the legend, the first striking detail is that Juan Diego heard beautiful music, which alone was enough to establish the heavenly origin of the Lady. For the Indians, music was the medium of divine communication. The Lady appeared on the sacred hill of Tepeyac, one of the four principal sacrificial sites in Mesoamerica. It was the sanctuary of Tonantzin, the Indian virgin mother of the gods. The dress was a pale red, the color of the spilled blood of sacrifices and the color of Huitzilopopchtli, the god who gave and preserved life. Indian blood had been spilled on Mexican soil and fertilized mother earth and now something new came forth. Red was also the color for the east, the direction from which the sun arose victorious after it had died for the night. The predominant color of the portrait is the blue-green of the mantle, which was the royal color of the Indian gods. It was also the color of Ometéotl, the origin of all natural forces. In the color psychology of the native world, blue-green stood at the center of the cross of opposing forces and signified the force unifying the opposing tensions at work in the world. One of the prophetic omens which the native wise men interpreted as a sign of the end of their civilization was the appearance, ten years before the conquest, of a large body of stars in the sky. The stars had been one of the signs of the end, and now the stars in her mantle announced the beginning of a new era. Being supported by heavenly creatures could have meant two, not necessarily contradictory, things. First, that she came on her own and, therefore, was not brought over by the Spaniards. Second, the Indians saw each period of time as supported by a god. This was recorded by a symbol representing the era being carried by a lesser creature. The Lady carried by heavenly creatures marked the appearance of a new era. She wore the black band of maternity around her waist, the sign that she was with child. This child was her offering to the New World. The Lady was greater than the greatest in the native pantheon because she hid the sun but did not extinguish it. Thus she was more powerful than the sun god, their principal deity. The Lady was also greater than their moon god, for she stood upon the moon, yet did not crush it. However, great as this Lady was, she was not a goddess. She wore no mask as the Indian gods did and her vibrant, compassionate face told anyone who looked upon it that she was the compassionate mother.

The fullness of the apparition developed with the Lady's request for a temple. In the Indian hieroglyphic recordings of the conquest, a burning, destroyed temple was the sign of the end of their civilization and way of life. Therefore, the request for the temple was not just for a building where her image could be venerated, but for a new way of life. It would express continuity with their past and yet radically transcend that past. One civilization had indeed ended, but now another one was erupting out of their own mother soil.

Not only did the Lady leave a powerful message in the image, but the credentials she chose to present herself to the New World were equally startling. For the bishop, the roses from the desert were a startling phenomenon; for the Indians, they were the sign of new life. Flowers and music to them were the supreme way of communication through which the presence of the invisible, all-powerful God could be expressed. As the apparition had begun with music, giving it an atmosphere of the divine, it reached its peak with flowers, the sign of life beyond life, the sign that beyond human suffering and death there was something greater-than-life in the dwelling place of the wonderful giver of life.[11]

The narration as it exists today does not appear to be historical, at least in the western scientific understanding of the word. It is not based on objective, verifiable, written documentation. However, it is a historical narrative to the people who have recorded their past through this specific literary genre.[12] Furthermore, popular religion has often been too easily labelled by outsiders, especially sociologists and theologians of the dominant groups, as alienating and superstitious of its very nature. Popular piety is not necessarily and of itself alienating; in fact, for a defeated, conquered and colonized people it serves as a final resistance against the way of the powerful. Popular religion becomes alienating when pastoral agents use it to legitimize and maintain the *status quo*. However, it becomes liberating when used as a source of unity and strength in the struggle for dignity and subsequent change against the powerful of society. It is the collective voice of the dominated people crying out: "We will not be eliminated; we will live on! We have been conquered, but we will not be destroyed." In the first stages it gives meaning to an otherwise meaningless existence and thus a reason for living. As the triumphant group has its way of recording history, so those who have been silenced by subjugation have their interpretation of the past. Their accounts exist in an even deeper way. For the defeated and powerless, history is recorded and lived in the collective memory of the people: their songs, dances, poetry, art, legends, and popular religion. For the powerful, history is only a written record, whereas for the defeated, history is life, for it is the memory that keeps telling them that things are not as they ought to be! This memory cannot be destroyed or opposed by the powerful because they do not understand it. Accordingly, it is not surprising that in the history of Mexico there is no place for the Tepeyac tradition. Guadalupe, the most persistent influence in Mexico, is found only in the folklore and popular religious practices of the masses.

At the time of the apparition, the Spanish were building churches over the ruins of the Aztec temples. The past grandeur and power of Tenochtitlán-Tlatelolco (the original name of present-day Mexico City) were being transformed into the glory of New Spain. Juan Diego dared to go to the center of power and with supernatural authority (as the Lady commanded) demanded that the powerful should change their plans and build a temple—a symbol of a new way of life—not within the grandeur of the city, in accordance with the plans of Spain, but within the *barriada* of Tepeyac in accordance with the desires of the people. The hero of the story is a simple conquered Indian from the *barriada* who is a symbol of the poor and oppressed refusing to be destroyed by the dominant group. This story's purpose was to convert the bishop, the symbol of the new Spanish power group, and to turn the attention of the conquering group from amassing wealth and power to the periphery of society where the people continued to live in poverty and misery.

The narration is only a wrapping for the continuing struggle of the masses for survival and liberation from the imposition of the ways of the powerful which has been going on for the past four hundred years. Through unceasing struggle, a dynamic tradition has emerged from the primitive story. This tradition has come to stand for the dignity, identity, unity, personal and collective emancipation, and the liberation movements of the Mexican people. Miguel Hidalgo fought for Mexican independence under the banner of Our Lady of Guadalupe. Emiliano Zapata led his agrarian reform under her protection. César Chávez battled against one of the most powerful economic blocks in the United States under the banner of Our Lady of Guadalupe and succeeded in his struggle for justice against all human odds. This tradition was relegated to the area of fable or legend not because it was lacking in historical veracity, but precisely because its living historical veracity cannot be fully accepted by the powerful political, economic, educational, sociological, or religious elite of any moment of history. The full truth of Tepeyac is the obvious disturbing truth of the millions of poor, powerless, peripheral oppressed of our society. Guadalupe's significance is the voice of the masses calling upon the elite to leave their economic, social, political, and religious thrones of pseudo-security and work with them—within the *movimientos de la base*—in transforming society into a more human place for everyone.

It was through the presence of Our Lady of Guadalupe that the possibility of cultural dialogue began. The missioners' activity had won a basis of authentic understanding, bringing to a climax their work of pre-evangelization. As at Bethlehem when the Son of God became man in Jesus and began the overthrow of the power of the Roman Empire, at Tepeyac Christ entered the soil of the Americas and began to reverse the European domination of the people in those lands. Tepeyac marks the beginning of the reconquest and the birth of Mexican Christianity.

It is from within the poor that the process of conversion is begun. The poor become the heralds of a new humanity. This critical challenge of our compassionate and liberating mother to

the powerful of any moment and place in the Americas continues today to be the dynamic voice and power of the poor and
oppressed of the Americas groaning and travailing for a more
human existence. Her presence is not a pacifier but an energizer
which gives meaning, dignity, and hope to the peripheral and
suffering people of today's societies. Her presence is the new
power of the powerless to triumph over the violence of the
powerful. In her, differences are assumed and the cathartic process of the cultural-religious encounter of Europe-America begins, but it has a long way to go. Nevertheless, it has begun and
is in process. This is the continuing miracle of Guadalupe—the
mother—queen of the Americas. Now the dream of the early
missioners, a new church and a New World, has definitely begun. The new people of the land would now be the *mestizo*
people—*la raza*—and the new Christianity would be neither the
cultural expression of Iberian Catholicism nor the mere continuation of the pre-Cortés religions of indigenous America, but a
new cultural expression of Christianity in the Americas.

Today theologians cannot afford to ignore the function and
meaning of popular religion for the popular masses.[13] A
theologian's task is not the canonization or rejection of the religious symbols of the people, but a continuous reinterpretation of
them in relation to the whole Gospel. In this way popular religion
will not be alienating but will help lead people to a deeper knowledge of the saving God. It will not be alienating or enslaving but
salvific and liberating. Popular religion which is regenerated (not
eliminated) by the Gospel becomes the invincible and efficacious
power of the powerless in their struggle for liberation.[14]

For millions of Mexicans and Mexican Americans of the United
States, Our Lady of Guadalupe is the temple in whom and through
whom Christ's saving presence is continually incarnated in the
soil of the Americas and it is through her mediation that:

> He shows strength with his arm,
> He scatters the proud in the imagination of their hearts.
> He puts down the mighty from their thrones,
> and exalts the oppressed.
> He fills the hungry with good things,
> and the rich he sends away empty handed.
> (Luke 1:51-52)

Notes

1. For an excellent exposition of this point in relation to the popular religion of Mexico, see J. Meyer, *La Cristiada* (Mexico, 1974) 316-323.

2. "Culture" is used here as all those solutions which a group finds in order to survive its natural and social situation. It is the complete world vision—norms, values, and rituals—of a group. Spain and Mexico had very highly developed cultures at the time of the clash.

3. Tepeyac is the hill north of Mexico City where the sanctuary of Tonantzin (which means "our mother")—the female aspect of the deity—was located. It was one of the most sacred pilgrimage sites of the Americas. Bernardino de Sahagún, *Historia general de las cosas de Nueva España* (Mexico, written in mid-1500s) 3:352.

4. "Mestizo" is the Spanish word for a person who is born from parents of different races. In contemporary Latin America it is acquiring a positive meaning, and the arrival of Columbus is celebrated as the day of *la raza* (the race), meaning the new race formed of Europe and Native America. There is no English translation of this concept, as the English word "half-breed" (a social rather than a biological term) is very derogatory and would have a completely different meaning.

5. For the first twelve missioners who came to Mexico, "New World" was a theological term indicating the place where the new Christianity was now to emerge. It would not be simply a continuation of the Christianity of Europe but a new, evangelical Christianity. S. Zavala, *Recuerdo de Vasco de Quiroga* (Mexico, 1965); Jacques Lafaye, *Quetzalcoatl et Guadalupe* (Paris, 1974) 52-67.

6. Some of the Native-American cultures were very well-developed and in many ways superior to those of sixteenth-century Europe. For a good description of this, see M. Leon-Portilla, *Aztec Thought and Culture* (Norman, Okla.: University of Oklahoma Press, 1963) esp. 134-176.

7. Octavio Paz, *The Labyrinth of Solitude* (New York, 1961) 93-96.

8. Leon-Portilla, *Aztec Thought and Culture* 74-79.

9. J. Soustelle, *La Vie quotidienne des Aztèques à la veille de la conquête espagnole* (Paris, 1955).

10. For a good description of the development of the Guadalupe tradition, see Lafaye, *Quetzalcoatl et Guadalupe* 281-396.

11. Leon-Portilla, *Aztec Thought and Culture* 102.

12. For a good example of a scholar who has been able to penetrate the historical consciousness alive in the folklore of the people, see N. Wachtel, *La Vision des vaincus* (Paris, 1971); Rodolfo Acuña, *Occupied America: A History of Chicanos* (New York: Harper & Row, 1981).

13. Pope Paul VI, *Evangelii Nuntiandi* (8 December 1975), sections 48 (on popular piety) and 63 (on adaptation and fidelity in expression). Meyer, *La Cristiada* 307 brings out the false way in which Mexican Catholicism has been judged by North-American and European missioners.

14. Meyer, *La Cristiada* 275-323.

4

Our Lady of Guadalupe Celebrations in San Antonio, Texas, 1840-1841

Timothy M. Matovina

On the 12th of December, the feast of Our Lady of Guadalupe, the patroness of Mexico, and of all the Spanish colonies, the inhabitants of San Antonio, who, in more prosperous times, solemnized this day with great rejoicings, felt their ancient zeal for the veneration of Mary revived . . .

With these words, Father Jean Marie Odin, a French Vincentian, began his description of the 1841 Our Lady of Guadalupe celebration in San Antonio, Texas. Impressed with the devotion expressed by San Antonians of Mexican or Spanish descent (Tejanos), Odin asserted that he had "seen few processions more edifying."[1]

To Odin, the future first ordinary of Texas, this celebration represented a devout and admirable expression of Marian piety among the Catholic population of San Antonio and the environs. For the predominately Tejano community of San Antonio, the Guadalupan feast was clearly of great significance, hence the careful planning of the celebration and the enthusiastic participation of the people.

The fervent Guadalupan devotion at San Antonio illustrates a religious and cultural tradition prevalent in various Mexican-descent communities during and after the U.S. conquest of what is now the southwest United States. From south Texas to Phoenix to the town of Monterey in northern California, local Hispanic communities celebrated Guadalupe and other Mexican Catholic rites despite their forced incorporation into a new nation and system of government.[2]

Faith expressions like Guadalupe celebrations are significant for liturgists and other pastoral agents. Studying these expressions in the deeper meanings they embody increases our understanding of the life experiences from which people's ritual emerges, for example, their devotional impulse and faith in divine providence, their collective memory of suffering, and their expression of communal identity in times of social change. It also enhances analysis of the societal structures reflected and, at times, transcended in ritual performances.

Analysis of faith expressions like Guadalupe celebrations requires attention to their ritual performance and the context in which they were enacted. Thus the full significance of the 1840-1841 Guadalupe celebrations for San Antonio Tejanos cannot be understood without first setting the historical context in which the celebrations took place, examining the celebrations themselves, and interpreting them in light of the context in which they were enacted.[3]

HISTORICAL CONTEXT

San Antonio de Béxar was part of the Spanish empire from that settlement's beginnings in the early eighteenth century until the time of Mexican independence (1821). For San Antonio, a century of Spanish rule was followed by a period of great unrest. While conflicts with Native Americans were prevalent throughout most of the settlement's history, during the first half of the nineteenth century battles at San Antonio between Spanish, Mexican, and later Texan military forces added to the violence suffered by the local populace. Incidents of hostility were one element of the historical context in which San Antonio Tejanos celebrated the Guadalupe feast in 1840 and 1841.

Important as the specific violent episodes were, the impact on the collective memory of San Antonio residents was greater. The cruelties of the War for Mexican Independence, for example, were recounted by eyewitnesses years afterwards. José Antonio Navarro recalled revolutionaries returning to San Antonio from the 1813 execution of the Spanish governor and his staff just outside the city, making public display of the "blood stained jewels" which were the spoils of the brutality of the executioners. When Spanish forces recaptured the city later that same year, Navarro witnessed the deaths of eighteen San Antonians who perished from suffocation in an inhuman confinement. Numerous others were killed by firing squad "for no more reason than that they had been accused of being in favor of independence."[4]

The battles fought in San Antonio during the Texas Revolution (1835-1836) also provided poignant memories for local residents. When Texan troops conquered the city in December 1835, house-to-house fighting with Mexican soldiers placed local residents in the midst of the conflict. During the battle the Texans broke through the walls of the houses with battering rams rather than risk the open streets. Later one soldier recalled "how the women and children would yell when we knocked the holes in the walls and went in."[5]

Three months later the famous Alamo battle took place. Among the Tejanos who remembered this battle was Enrique Esparza, who stated that "neither age nor infirmity could make me forget [the battle], for the scene was one of such horror that it could never be forgotten by anyone who witnessed its incidents." Eulalia Yorba, a Tejana eyewitness, later commented:

> The morning of Sunday—the 6th of March [the day of the Alamo battle]—ah! indeed, I could never forget that, even if I lived many years more . . . I used to try when I was younger to describe that awful sight [the aftermath of the battle], but I never could find sufficient language.

Esparza, Yorba, and others also recalled the horrors in San Antonio after the battle: the sufferings of the wounded, the incineration of the bodies of the Alamo defenders at General Antonio López de Santa Anna's orders, and the disposal of corpses in the San Antonio River because the numerous deceased Mexican soldiers made it impossible to bury them all.[6]

Contemporary diaries, memoirs, and correspondence of San Antonians and travelers are filled with descriptions of the frequent conflicts with Comanches in and around San Antonio at this time. As Father Odin wrote in an 1841 letter: "There is not a family [in San Antonio] who does not mourn the death of a father, of a son, of a brother, or of a spouse pitilessly slaughtered by the Comanches." A resident of San Antonio told Odin that within the first ten months of 1840 thirty-five Tejanos and fourteen Anglo Americans had been killed by the Comanches in or near the city.[7]

The "Court House fight" is perhaps the most noteworthy of these conflicts with the Comanches. On 19 March 1840 representatives of the Comanches and the Texas government met at the San Antonio Court House. Disagreements about the return of prisoners held by the Comanches resulted in violence between the two delegations. This fight escalated and the entire town was drawn into the *melee*. Official reports state that thirty-five Native Americans were killed, along with six Anglo Americans and one Mexican.[8] Occurring just a short time before the 1840-1841 Guadalupe feasts, this battle as well as other conflicts formed a part of San Antonians' collective memory at the time of these celebrations.

Another element in the historical context of these celebrations was the negative views many Anglo Americans held of Tejanos. Tejano Catholicism was frequently an important element of their critiques. An 1828 visitor to San Antonio concluded that the inhabitants were "completely the slaves of Popish Superstition and despotism" and that "the religion of this place is understood by very few if any as a gracious affection of the heart and soul but a mere requisition of personal mortification in [the] form of penances[,] etc." Another visitor claimed in 1837 that, at San Antonio,

> Every Mexican professes to be a Catholic and carries about his person the crucifix, the rosary, and other symbols of the mother church. But religion with him, if one is permitted to judge of the feelings of the heart by outward signs, is more a habit than a principle or feeling.

Baptist minister Z.N. Morrell stated that the religious practices of San Antonio Catholics during his 1839 visit exemplified "the blindest superstition." Presbyterian minister William L. McCalla, who visited San Antonio in 1840, decried the local customs of holy day festivities and *fandangos* (dances) as evidence of Catholicism's corrupting influence and prayed that Protestant emissaries would reclaim Texas from "the mother and mistress of all churches."[9]

Anglo Americans also accused Tejanos of being traitors to the cause of Texas. In December 1835, Governor Henry Smith warned General Edward Burleson not to trust the "false friends" among San Antonio Tejanos during the Texan siege of their city. A month later Doctor Amos Pollard warned Smith from San Antonio about "our most formidable foe—our internal enemy—The mexican tory party of the country." Colonel William Barret Travis wrote a letter from the Alamo declaring all San Antonians who had not joined him there "public enemies." While some accusations of Tejano loyalty to Mexico were true, Anglo Americans tended to identify all Tejanos as enemies of the Republic of Texas. [10]

These accusations of Tejano disloyalty continued even after the Revolution. In November 1836 a press report in a Texas newspaper labeled Tejanos who remained at San Antonio "pretended friends" of Texas. An 1837 visitor observed that "a small military force is stationed at San Antonio to prevent treasonable intercourse with the inhabitants beyond the Rio Grande."[11]

Anglo-American critiques of Tejano religious practices and suspicions of Tejano political allegiance to Mexico led some to conclude that the two groups had irreconcilable religious and cultural differences. Major Jonas Harrison epitomized such claims when he declared in December 1835 that "the anglo Americans and the Mexicans, if not primitively a different people, habit, education, and religion, have made them essentially so. The two people cannot mingle together."[12]

Yet another element in the historical context of the 1840-1841 San Antonio Guadalupe celebrations was the changing leadership within the Catholic Church. In 1840 Texas was removed from the Mexican diocese of Linares and declared a prefecture apostolic under the diocese of New Orleans. Vincentian Father John Timon was appointed prefect apostolic, but was unable to assume the responsibility personally because of other duties within his congregation. He sent his French confrere, Father Jean Marie Odin, as vice prefect apostolic instead.

This shift in ecclesiastical jurisdiction led to a change in clergy at San Antonio's San Fernando parish. Four months before the 1840 Guadalupe celebration, Odin removed the two native priests at San Antonio, Padres Refugio de la Garza and José Antonio Valdéz, claiming that their ministry was ineffective and that they had broken their priestly vows by having wives and children. In their place he appointed his Spanish confrere Miguel Calvo as pastor of San Fernando.[13]

Some foreign priests who encountered Tejanos for the first time opined that their knowledge and practice of the faith were inadequate. Timon stated that "the poor Mexicans would die for their religion, yet they hardly knew what their religion was; how could they? Their faith was rather a divine instinct that grew from their baptism, than a faith of knowledge." Recalling his first years in Texas, Odin later wrote that the Catholic population he encountered "kept no more than a slight vestige of faith."[14]

Catholic clergy were certainly not as critical of Tejano Catholicism as Protestant ministers were of Tejano religious practices. As was previously mentioned, Odin participated in Tejano religious feasts like the 1841 San Antonio Guadalupe celebration and, in contrast to other statements about Tejanos' lack of faith, spoke enthusiastically of the religious zeal demonstrated in those celebrations. Many priests also made heroic efforts to serve the Spanish-speaking segment of their flock. Odin, for example, learned Spanish and was insistent that those coming to minister in Texas do the same. Calvo's Vincentian confreres later claimed that, during his twelve years as pastor of San Fernando (1840-1852), he "consoled and defended the native-born [Tejanos] against the cruelty of the yankees."[15]

But foreign clergy's lack of familiarity with local traditions meant Tejano leaders had to assume much of the responsibility for continuing those traditions. While local leaders had organized communal celebrations since the eighteenth century, frequently they had done so in conjunction with clergy like Father de la Garza who were accustomed to Tejano feasts and practices. Odin and Calvo may have been familiar with feasts like Our Lady of Guadalupe,[16] but some local practices in celebrating these feasts were undoubtedly new to them. Practices which were retained through the initiative of San Antonio Tejanos are significant because they indicate traditions that the local community valued enough to maintain.

The prior history of Guadalupan devotion in San Antonio was a final element in the historical context of the 1840-1841 San Antonio Guadalupe celebrations. Although some antecedents are found in the San Antonio missions, the primary sources of Guadalupan devotion in San Antonio were diocesan clergy and the parishioners of the settlement's first parish, San Fernando.

Eighteenth-century inventories indicate that only one of the five San Antonio missions had an image of Our Lady of Guadalupe, the mission of San José y San Miguel de Aguayo. This was probably because it was the only San Antonio mission founded by friars from the College of Our Lady of Guadalupe at Zacatecas. The missions were outside of the town and under the ecclesiastical jurisdiction of the friars who ran them. Civilian town residents and some military personnel belonged to San Fernando parish; their public devotion to Our Lady of Guadalupe was prevalent from at least the mid-1750s.[17]

The first patronesses of San Fernando parish were those of the civilian settlers and soldiers in the area: Nuestra Señora de la Candelaria and Nuestra Señora de Guadalupe. As the Canary Islander civilians interacted with the settlement's other cultural groups through the end of the eighteenth century, a regional Tejano identity emerged, however, an identity to which the indigenous Guadalupe had more appeal. Guadalupe thus enjoyed greater prominence than la Candelaria in the ritual life of the local populace. By the time of Texas independence in 1836 the conflated December celebration of the Immaculate Conception, Guadalupe, and Christmas had been the principal feast in San Antonio for decades. The Guadalupe image had become the Mexican national symbol; the Tejano population of San Antonio celebrated her feast with the enthusiasm evidenced in other areas of the Republic.[18]

Like other celebrations at San Antonio, social divisions in the local community were reflected in the Guadalupan festivities. Under Spanish and Mexican rule, town council members and other prominent lay leaders organized the celebrations. Citizens selected to plan a given feast were expected to make financial contributions. This requirement tended to limit participation on official planning committees to wealthier residents, who would then occupy positions of prominence during communal celebrations. Sometimes two simultaneous dances were held in connection with a celebration, separating the wealthy from the general populace.[19]

DESCRIPTION

Two accounts of the 1840-1841 Guadalupan celebrations from primary sources are extant. One, contained in a letter of Father

Odin (cited in part above), describes the 1841 celebration; the other, taken from the memoirs of Mary A. Maverick, who was Protestant, provides an account of the celebration in 1840.[20]

In both Odin's and Maverick's descriptions the most noteworthy activity mentioned is the Guadalupe processions. Maverick describes one procession, Odin two (one in the afternoon and the other in the evening). Although there are minor discrepancies between the two accounts, there is enough agreement to suggest some general patterns for the ritual performance of the processions. An elegantly adorned image of Our Lady of Guadalupe was the principal ritual object. Odin also mentions a cross, banner of Mary, and the decoration of the church with ornaments offered by local women for this purpose. Priests and the general populace both took part in the processions, including a number of Anglo Americans who Odin claims came from as far away as Austin (about eighty miles). Young girls dressed in white and bearing candles (some had flowers according to Odin) were the immediate attendants of the Guadalupan image. Maverick adds that fiddlers also participated, Odin that sixty members of the militia served as escorts. The rosary was prayed, and according to Odin religious hymns honoring the mother of God were sung. Both observers recall guns being fired off as part of the devotion, and Odin writes of cannons and bells sounding as well. They also mention religious ceremonies at San Fernando church in addition to the processions.

Maverick's account states that the procession "proceeded through the squares and some of the principal streets" before finally arriving at San Fernando. Although Odin does not mention the route of the afternoon procession, he indicates that in the evening it went around the two main plazas on either side of the church. In both descriptions, then, the entourage passed some of the houses of the city, as well as the two main plazas. They also went by the Court House (site where the battle with the Comanches began in March 1840), and of course in both cases San Fernando church itself was prominent.

Significantly, these buildings could have easily brought to mind recent events from San Antonio's past. In describing the physical appearance of the town, various travelers commented on the signs of battle still visible on houses and public buildings. One visitor remarked:

The military squares, of which there are two, have been [at various times] heaped with the slain. The houses that surround the square, and the church, which occupies the center are perforated by hundreds of musket and cannon shot . . . numerous heaps of ruins both in the town & neighborhood marke [sic] the places where houses once stood. Ruined walls, hedges, ditches, and artificial channels, some of which are dry, but though many bright streams of watter [sic] trickling along, with here and their [sic] some flowering shrub, or wounded and dying fig or peach tree, standing on these borders, tell us in language not to be mistaken of a once industrious, wealthy, and to a great degree refined and civilized population.[21]

Thus the setting for the Guadalupe celebrations bore the marks of events from the city's past: battles and conquests, conflicts with the Native Americans, former times of tranquillity and prosperity, perhaps even the memory of loved ones who had been killed on the route of the Guadalupe procession.

Like the setting of the celebrations, some of the participants could have served as reminders of the city's past. Consider, for example, the following comment of British traveler William Bollaert from his 1843 visit to San Antonio: "There are a few Comanche children in San Antonio; on asking one, a boy who was assisting a stone mason in the Plaza, how and when he came there, he replied, pointing to the Court House, 'My father was killed there'; but, he appeared gay and happy."[22] No doubt brothers and sisters, daughters and sons, former companions of a loved one, and others brought back past memories as easily as this Comanche child would have.

Odin's account states that both men and women were involved in preparing for the celebrations. As was previously mentioned, the assignment of foreign clergy to San Antonio in 1840 necessitated that Tejano leaders assume responsibility for continuing local traditions. According to Odin, Tejanos did this by purchasing gun powder to fire salutes as an expression of devotion, while Tejanas collected jewelry and other ornaments used in the decoration of the church and the Guadalupan image.

Both Odin and Maverick indicate a general participation of the San Antonio populace in the religious ceremonies. However, Maverick notes that after the ceremony at San Fernando "the more prominent families[,] taking the Patroness along with them, adjourned to Mr. José Flores' house on [the] west side of Military Plaza, where they danced most of the night." Since only a few Anglo-American families lived in San Antonio at the time, this statement refers to families of Mexican (or Spanish) descent. Thus, while all San Antonians were welcome to the procession and prayer service of the Guadalupe celebration, in the dance which accompanied them the upper class seemingly exercised some prerogatives over the general populace.

Anglo Americans, both residents of the city and visitors from elsewhere, apparently were not excluded. Maverick recounts that she and her family were invited to the public celebration and the gathering at the Flores residence in 1840, while Odin wrote that a number of Anglo Americans from Austin and the surrounding areas attended in 1841. Their presence illustrates San Antonio Tejano efforts to include Anglo Americans in their public celebrations during the period of the Texas Republic.[23]

INTERPRETATION

The foregoing description of the 1840-1841 San Antonio Guadalupe celebrations and treatment of their historical context elucidate a multi-layered interpretation of these celebrations. First, for the ritual subjects of these celebrations, the processions and religious services were obviously a means of offering devotion and invoking the intercession of their patroness. Legends current among San Antonians at that time evidence a pattern of petitioning and receiving divine intervention in time of need.[24] Religious processions held in 1833 had the expressed intention of seeking divine aid from a cholera epidemic. A contemporary account asserted that the Guadalupe image had induced flood waters to recede on the San Antonio River.[25] Clearly, the Guadalupe rituals were a religious activity intended to venerate the mother of the Mexican people and follow in this tradition of supplication for celestial assistance and protection.

The Guadalupe celebrations could also be understood as the "sacralisation of space," as Latin American theologian Enrique Düssel explains:

> Processions, and above all pilgrimages are a "road" through profane space towards the centrality of the consecrated space *par excellence*, the shrine of the Virgin of Guadalupe,

those of Copacabana, the Christ of "Gran Poder" or Esquipula. As long as the religious practice lasts, for a short time there is some control over the space of "transition," which may be hostile but is now controlled by the people. The people occupies and controls space by its number, and so simultaneously achieves self-affirmation.[26]

Given the people's collective memory of the Alamo, the Court House fight, and other battles and conflicts, the Guadalupe processions functioned as an attempt to consecrate anew space which had been violated by so many violent episodes. The reminders of these past events in the bullet marks, damage done to buildings, other signs of destruction, even in the faces of Comanche children and others in the town, only augment the sense that these processions served as purification rites for a violated city and its people. The ritual itself was filled with signs of symbolic reversal: jewelry and valuable ornaments were not robbed or destroyed but freely given or loaned for the celebration, music replaced previous cries of anguish, guns and cannons were used for devotion rather than violence, young girls led a procession down the same streets on which they had fled from hostilities. Intentionally or not, these rituals strove for purification or sacralisation, a part of the process which enabled San Antonio Tejanos to endure despite all their suffering.

These celebrations also functioned as a means to express identity in a time of social change. Separation from Mexico removed Tejanos from formal political alliance with others of Mexican heritage, and raised the question of whether they would abandon that heritage altogether. Anglo Americans critiqued Tejano religious practice as superstitious and superficial and frequently claimed that Tejanos retained Mexican ways and loyalties. In the face of these Anglo-American attitudes and suspicions, Tejano initiative to continue the Guadalupe ritual expressed their resistance to the diminishment of their religious and cultural heritage: it continued a devotion prevalent in San Antonio from the early years of the settlement's history and it was performed in the Mexican way of a colorful procession with flowers, candles, elaborate decorations adorning the Guadalupe image and the church, and the sound of bells, cannons, and guns. The celebration of the Guadalupe feast after Texas independence showed that the continuing presence of San Antonio

Tejanos in their Texas homeland did not indicate a rejection of their Mexican heritage. But Anglo Americans were also included in the celebrations, demonstrating that native-born San Antonians were not sustaining a Tejano enclave which was hostile to its new neighbors within the Republic of Texas. Thus while Tejanos adapted to a new political order under the Texas Republic, Anglo Americans at San Antonio were drawn into the Tejano circle of public celebrations and accommodated themselves to a community that retained its Mexican Catholic flavor.

The 1840-1841 Guadalupe celebrations also reinforced existing social structures on class lines but transcended those structures on gender lines. On the one hand, in these celebrations Tejana (women's) participation evidenced a marked contrast to their usual position of subordination. Admittedly, their leadership role was limited to collecting jewelry and other ornaments for the decoration of the church and the Guadalupan image. But young Tejanas also occupied a prominent place within the sacred space of worship. They served in the religious processions as the immediate attendants of the Guadalupan image, which was the principal ritual object. Such prominence was not evident in other areas of Tejana life. Women were denied the vote and the right to hold office. They could be forced by law to stay with their husbands. Often they suffered harsh legal penalties for adultery, while men frequently received no legal reprisal for the same offense. Their subservient position was symbolized in social life by the custom of wives eating separately from their husbands, but only after having served the men their meal.[27] In a society that obviously kept women subordinate to men, the relative prominence of Tejanas in the planning of these celebrations and in accompanying their patroness as attendants is striking.

Tejana prominence in these celebrations can be better understood within the context of women's role in Latin American Catholicism. Ana María Díaz-Stevens has argued that, despite the patriarchy of institutional Catholicism and Latin American societies, women within those societies have exercised autonomous authority in the devotional life of their people. Women's leadership outside of official church structures constitutes the "matriarchal core" of Latin American Catholicism. This view is consistent with the prominence of Tejanas in San Antonio's Guadalupe celebrations, who apparently found in Guadalupan devotion a means of participation in communal life frequently denied them by the structures of the political and legal systems, social life, and the institutional life of the church.[28]

While a more egalitarian relationship between the sexes was evident in the Guadalupe celebrations, they also reinforced existing class divisions in San Antonio society, as similar celebrations had done during the Spanish and Mexican periods. Maverick recounts that the Guadalupan image used in religious ceremonies was taken to a dance held by "the more prominent families." While the Guadalupe procession and prayer service expressed an equality of invitation, the continuation of the celebration in evening festivities divided the poor and the more prominent. The status of the latter was reinforced by removing to their dance the principal ritual object used in religious services.

These class divisions illustrate what David Montejano has called a "peace structure." By "peace structure" Montejano refers to "a general postwar arrangement that allows the victors to maintain law and order without the constant use of force." A primary element in this structure was "an accommodation between the victorious Anglos and the defeated Mexican elite." This accommodation did not substantially alter the traditional authority structures of Tejano society, but rather placed Anglo Americans atop the existing hierarchy. Significantly, the Mavericks' social circle included prominent Tejano families such as the Navarros, Sotos, Garzas, Garcías, Zambranos, Seguíns, Veramendis, and Yturris; Mary Maverick wrote in 1838 that "our only society are Mexicans." In 1839 an overwhelmingly Tejano electorate voted Samuel Maverick mayor of San Antonio. The Mavericks' social status and political success are consistent with the concept of peace structure outlined by Montejano. Their participation in Guadalupe festivities at the Flores' residence reflects their incorporation as influential Anglo Americans into the Tejano inner circle.[29]

The 1840-1841 San Antonio Guadalupe celebrations also reflect the contemporary Tejano conviction that loyalty to Texas and their Mexican heritage were compatible. When asked in later years if he loved Texas more than Mexico, San Antonio resident Enrique Esparza stated that he was of mixed Indian and Spanish blood, and "proud of that ancestry." He then added that he saw his father "die for Texas" in the Alamo battle and that he was "proud to be a Texan and an American." In 1843 twelve Mexican soldiers from Santa Anna's army who elected to remain in Texas stated that "we consider ourselves as Freemen and Texians, by adoption—willing [and] ready at any moment to defend this soil." But they went on to add, "We do not deny being Mexicans, far from it."[39] The Guadalupe celebrations were a ritual expression of Tejano identity as a people of Mexican Catholic heritage who were adapting to life among Anglo Americans in the Republic of Texas.

Above all, the Guadalupe celebrations illustrate Tejanos' devotional impulse and their penchant for intercessory prayer. Faced with needs such as enduring despite a collective memory of suffering, San Antonians' Guadalupan devotion expressed their plea for divine aid. In making this prayer, Tejanos implicitly sought to understand events like the violent episodes which had beset them. Anthropologist Clifford Geertz has claimed:

> The Problem of Meaning in each of its intergrading aspects . . . is a matter of affirming, or at least recognizing, the inescapability of ignorance, pain, and injustice on the human plane while simultaneously denying that these irrationalities are characteristic of the world as a whole. And it is in terms of religious symbolism, a symbolism relating man's [sic] sphere of existence to a wider sphere within which it is conceived to rest, that both the affirmation and the denial are made.[31]

In celebrating the feast of their principal patroness, Tejanos placed their plight within a wider context of meaning. By processing with their patroness past the sites of recent violence, for example, they recalled the community's suffering while denying that their celestial mother would forego responding to their misery.

CONCLUSION

Virgilio Elizondo has argued that "were it not for Our Lady of Guadalupe there would be no Mexican or Mexican-American people today." Elizondo also contends that "the significance of Guadalupe, far from being a pacifier, is a dynamic call to action and a powerful symbol for the unification of a people."[32]

This study substantiates Elizondo's claims about Our Lady of Guadalupe's central role for the life and collective identity of Mexican-American communities. The symbol of Guadalupe enabled San Antonio Tejanos to endure a collective memory of suffering and resist attitudes that would diminish their religious and cultural heritage. While more prominent members of the community separated themselves from the general populace at evening festivities, the preceding processions and prayer services evidenced an equality of invitation that unified Anglo Americans and Tejanos of all social classes in a common act of worship. The celebrations also transcended in some ways the subservient role of Tejanas in that society, especially through the alternative model for gender relations exemplified by young Tejanas occupying a prominent place within the sacred space of ritual. As the principal patroness of the San Antonio Tejano community, Our Lady of Guadalupe provided a symbolic link with the past that enabled that community to confront present upheaval with faith. She also engendered hope for a future in which relations within the community and beyond it would reflect the dignity of all people as daughters and sons of a loving mother.

Notes

1. Jean Marie Odin to Jean-Baptiste Étienne, 7 February 1842, in *The United States Catholic Magazine and Monthly Review* 3 (October 1844) 729. A copy of this letter is in the Catholic Archives of Texas, Austin (CAT).

2. See, e.g., Abbé [Emanuel] Domenech, *Missionary Adventures in Texas and Mexico: A Personal Narrative of Six Years' Sojourn in Those Regions* (London: Longman, Brown, Green, Longmans, and Roberts, 1858) 357-359; Bradford Luckingham, *Minorities in Phoenix: A Profile of Mexican American, Chinese American, and African American Communities, 1860-1992* (Tucson: University of Arizona Press, 1994) 19; Walter Colton, *Three Years in California: Together with Excerpts from the Author's Deck and Port, Covering His Arrival in California and a Selection of his Letters from Monterey*, with an introduction by Marguerite Eyer Wilbur (Stanford: Stanford University Press, 1949) 224.

3. The methodology employed in this chapter is based on the work of anthropologist Victor Turner, which provides helpful models for interpreting rituals within their larger context. See, e.g., Victor Turner, *The Forest of Symbols: Aspects of Ndembu Ritual* (Ithaca: Cornell University

Press, 1967); Turner, *Dramas, Fields, and Metaphors: Symbolic Action in Human Society* (Ithaca: Cornell University Press, 1974); Edith Turner, ed., *On the Edge of the Bush: Anthropology as Experience* (Tucson: University of Arizona Press, 1985).

4. José Antonio Navarro, *Apuntes históricos interesantes de San Antonio de Béxar escritos por el C. Dn. José Antonio Navarro, en noviembre de 1853. Y publicados por varios de sus amigos* (San Antonio: Privately printed, 1869) 16, 18. Recollections of these events from other San Antonians include Antonio Menchaca, *Memoirs* (San Antonio: Yanaguana Society, 1937) 13-19; J[osé] M[aría] Rodríguez, *Rodríguez Memoirs of Early Texas* (San Antonio: Passing Show Printing, 1913; reprint, San Antonio: Standard, 1961) 59. Quotations are author's translation of the text.

5. Sion R. Bostick, "Reminiscences of Sion R. Bostick," *Quarterly of the Texas State Historical Association* 5 (October 1901) 89-90.

6. "Alamo's Only Survivor," *San Antonio Express,* 12 May 1907, 14; "Another Story of the Alamo," *San Antonio Express,* 12 April 1896, 13. For other Tejano Alamo accounts, see Timothy M. Matovina, *The Alamo Remembered: Tejano Accounts and Perspectives* (Austin: University of Texas Press, 1995).

7. Odin to Étienne, 11 April 1841, CAT (quotation); Odin, "Daily Journal" (photocopy) 10, CAT. Descriptions of Native-American conflicts by San Antonio residents include Rodríguez, *Memoirs* 26-29, 34, 64; Rena Maverick Green, ed., *Memoirs of Mary A. Maverick* (San Antonio: Alamo, 1921) 18-20, 25-37, 42-51.

8. *Austin Texas Sentinel* 23, 25 March, 15 April 1840; *Houston Telegraph and Texas Register,* 8 April 1840. Although there are no written Comanche accounts, some travelers through San Antonio claimed that the Texas delegation acted treacherously, e.g., Prince Carl of Solms-Braunfels, *Texas, 1844-45,* trans. from the German (Houston: Anson Jones, 1936) 42. A Catholic priest even records this opinion based on a companion's conversation with the Comanches. Domenech, *Missionary Adventures in Texas and Mexico* 120-121.

9. J.C. Clopper, "J.C. Clopper's Journal and Book of Memoranda for 1828," *Quarterly of the Texas State Historical Association* 13 (July 1909) 72, 76; Andrew Forest Muir, ed., *Texas in 1837: An Anonymous, Contemporary Narrative* (Austin: University of Texas Press, 1988) 103; Z.N. Morrell, *Flowers and Fruits from the Wilderness; or, Thirty-six Years in Texas and Two Winters in Honduras* (Boston: Gould and Lincoln, 1872) 118; W.L. McCalla, *Adventures in Texas, Chiefly in the Spring and Summer of 1840* (Philadelphia: Privately printed, 1841) 81-83.

10. Henry Smith to Edward Burleson, 9 December 1835, in *Official Correspondence of the Texan Revolution, 1835-1836,* ed. William C. Binkley (New York: D. Appleton-Century, 1936) 1:177; Amos Pollard to Smith, 16 January 1836, in ibid., 1:300; William Barret Travis to President of Convention, 3 March 1836, in the *San Felipe de Austin* (later *Houston*) *Telegraph and Texas Register,* 12 March 1836.

11. *Columbia* (later *Houston*) *Telegraph and Texas Register*, 9 November 1836; Muir, ed., *Texas in 1837* 107.

12. J[onas] Harrison, "Address Favoring Declaration of Independence," 22 December 1835, in *The Papers of Mirabeau Buonaparte Lamar*, ed. Charles Adams Gulick, Jr., and Katherine Elliott (Austin: Von Boeckmann-Jones, 1973) 1:270.

13. Odin's dismissal of the native clergy is treated in Timothy M. Matovina, *Tejano Religion and Ethnicity: San Antonio, 1821-1860* (Austin: University of Texas Press, 1995) 42-43.

14. John Timon, "Narrative of the Barrens" (photocopy) 39, Vincentian Archives, St. Mary's of the Barrens, Perryville, Missouri; Odin to Propagation of the Faith, 28 March 1852, CAT.

15. Odin to Anthony Blanc, 12 December 1852, CAT; Odin to John Baptist Purcell, 25 June 1861, The University of Notre Dame Archives, South Bend Ind.; Miguel Joaquín Calvo, Fichero de personal, Archivo Matritense C.M., Madrid (quotation). Quotation is author's translation of the text.

16. Papal recognition had been given to the Guadalupan image in 1754, when Benedict XIV proclaimed her the patroness of New Spain and declared 12 December her feast day.

17. Jesús Francisco de la Teja, *San Antonio de Béxar: A Community on New Spain's Northern Frontier* (Albuquerque: University of New Mexico Press, 1995) 148-149. For inventory reports of Guadalupan images at the San José mission, see Friar Ildefonso Marmolejo, "Inventory and Report of San José," 4 October 1755, in *The San José Papers: The Primary Sources of the History of Mission San José y San Miguel de Aguayo*, comp. Marion A. Habig (San Antonio: Old Spanish Missions Historical Research Library, 1978-1990) 1:108; Habig, *The Alamo Chain of Missions: A History of San Antonio's Five Old Missions* (Chicago: Franciscan Herald Press, 1976) 99.

18. Timothy M. Matovina, "New Frontiers of Guadalupanismo," *Journal of Hispanic/Latino Theology* 5 (August 1997) 20–36; Gerald E. Poyo and Gilberto M. Hinojosa, eds., *Tejano Origins in Eighteenth-Century San Antonio* (Austin: University of Texas Press, 1991) esp. 140; Jacques Lafaye, *Quetzalcoatl and Guadalupe: The Formation of Mexican National Consciousness, 1531-1813* (Chicago: University of Chicago Press, 1976). The importance of the December celebrations at San Antonio is evidenced in the preparations made for them. See, e.g., Manuel de Salcedo to People of Béxar, 2 December 1810, in Walter Prescott Webb, "Christmas and New Year in Texas," *Southwestern Historical Quarterly* 44 (January 1941) 358-359; [*ayuntamiento*] [town council] to [Mariano Varela], 5 October 1815, Béxar Archives, Center for American History, University of Texas, Austin (CAH); Juan Seguín to Béxar *alcalde* [mayor], 2 December 1834, ibid.; "Minutes of the City Council of the City of San Antonio, Spanish Minute Books One and Two" (typescript), 31 October 1816, 2-3 December 1830, 1 December

1831, 6 December 1832, 5 December 1833, CAH. See also Jesús F. de la Teja and John Wheat, "Béxar: Profile of a Tejano Community, 1820-1832," *Southwestern Historical Quarterly* 89 (July 1985) 23.

19. De la Teja, *San Antonio de Béxar* 132, 148-149. During the 1829 independence day celebrations at San Antonio, two dances were held, "a great ball" and "a minor dance at another place for the entertainment of the public." Minutes of the junta for the Independence Day celebration, 12 September 1829, in De la Teja and Wheat, "Béxar: Profile of a Tejano Community," 22-23. The testimony of city residents and visitors during the period of the Texas Republic indicate that social divisions continued among San Antonio Tejanos. Matovina, *Tejano Religion and Ethnicity* 26.

20. Odin to Étienne, 7 February 1842; Green, ed., *Memoirs of Mary A. Maverick* 53-54.

21. William A. McClintock, "Journal of a Trip Through Texas and Northern Mexico in 1846-1847," *Southwestern Historical Quarterly* 34 (October 1930) 146-147.

22. W. Eugene Hollon and Ruth Lapham Butler, eds., *William Bollaert's Texas* (Norman: University of Oklahoma Press, 1956) 229-230.

23. Tejanos welcomed newcomers to San Antonio at other local festivities after Texas independence. The popular *fandangos* (dances), for example, were frequented by numerous recent arrivals to the city. Matovina, *Tejano Religion and Ethnicity* 45.

24. One such legend "believed by all the old Mexicans about San Antonio" described the miraculous escape of a priest from the Comanches by the parting of river waters "as the Red sea [sic] did for the Israelites of old." George William Bonnell, *Topographical Description of Texas. To Which Is Added, An Account of the Indian Tribes* (Austin: Clark, Wing, & Brown, 1840; reprint, Waco: Texian Press, 1964) 82-83. Another story of providential escape from Native-American attack, along with a legend about the origin of the San Antonio River, appear in Charles Merritt Barnes, *Combats and Conquests of Immortal Heroes* (San Antonio: Guessaz & Ferlet, 1910) 76-81. These were based on the recollections of San Antonio resident Antonio Menchaca.

25. The 1833 processions are described in Benjamin Lundy, *The Life, Travels and Opinions of Benjamin Lundy, Including His Journeys to Texas and Mexico; with a Sketch of Contemporary Events, and a Notice of the Revolution in Hayti* (Philadelphia: William D. Parrish, 1847; reprint, New York: Negro Universities Press, 1969) 53-55. For the claim that the Guadalupe image saved San Antonio from a flood, see Sisters Mary Patrick Joseph and Mary Augustine Joseph to Mr. Walshe and family, 16 December 1852, in *Letters from the Ursuline, 1852-1853*, ed. Catherine McDowell (San Antonio: Trinity University Press, 1977)

273. The letter does not give the date of this reported occurrence, but suggests it was several years earlier.

26. Enrique Düssel, "Popular Religion as Oppression and Liberation: Hypotheses on Its Past and Present in Latin America," in *Popular Religion*, ed. Norbert Greinacher and Norbert Mette (Edinburgh: T. & T. Clark, 1986) 89.

27. David J. Weber, *The Mexican Frontier, 1821-1846: The American Southwest Under Mexico* (Albuquerque: University of New Mexico Press, 1982) 215-216. Weber's analysis shows that frontier conditions afforded women greater potential for upward social mobility than their counterparts in central Mexico. But he also demonstrates that the structures of politics, the legal system, and social life kept women subservient.

28. Ana María Díaz-Stevens, "The Saving Grace: The Matriarchal Core of Latino Catholicism," *Latino Studies Journal* 4 (September 1993) 60-78.

29. David Montejano, *Anglos and Mexicans in the Making of Texas, 1836-1986* (Austin: University of Texas Press, 1987) 34 (first two quotations); Mary A. Maverick to Agatha S. Adams, 25 August 1838, in *Samuel Maverick, Texan: 1803-1870: A Collection of Letters, Journals and Memoirs*, ed. Rena Maverick Green (San Antonio: Privately printed, 1952) 77 (third quotation); Green, ed., *Memoirs of Mary A. Maverick* 54; "Minutes of the City Council of the City of San Antonio from 1837 to 1849, Journal A" (typescript) 33, CAH.

30. "Esparza, the Boy of the Alamo, Remembers," in *Rise of the Lone Star: A Story of Texas Told by Its Pioneers*, ed. Howard R. Driggs and Sarah S. King (New York: Frederick A. Stokes, 1936) 214-215; Bernardo Arze, Francisco Albares, José Morillo, and others to Editor, *Houston Morning Star*, 10 October 1843.

31. Clifford Geertz, "Religion as a Cultural System," in *The Interpretation of Cultures: Selected Essays by Clifford Geertz* (New York: Basic Books, 1973) 108.

32. Virgilio Elizondo, "Popular Religion as Support of Identity; A Pastoral-Psychological Case-Study Based on the Mexican American Experience in the USA," in *Popular Religion*, ed. Greinacher and Mette 39; Elizondo, *La Morenita: Evangelizer of the Americas* (San Antonio: Mexican American Cultural Center Press, 1980) 90. The former reference is the second essay in this collection.

PART THREE

Celebrating the Sacred

Introduction

THE GREAT FEASTS OF THE CHURCH DO NOT ONLY COMMEMORATE FOR
them the wonders of God's love and mercy; no, they bring
the great events of Christ's life and of His saints to the very
doors of their hearts. In their vivid imagination Christ,
lying in the cold manger of Bethlehem, or Christ hanging
bruised and bleeding on the cross, is present before them:
they see Him; they hear Him; they touch Him; they speak
with Him.
> —Archbishop Arthur J. Drossaerts, comment on
> Mexican-descent faithful of San Antonio, 1929

When I walked behind Jesus on the Way of the Cross I
wondered what I would have done had I been there. The
people of San Fernando drew me into the passion and put
me right there with Jesus.
> —Pastor Buckner Fanning,
> Trinity Baptist Church, San Antonio

The church has a long and varied history of ministry in cross-
cultural settings. Ministerial efforts in Mexico and among Mexican Americans and other Hispanics in the United States are a
chapter in that history which influences those communities dra-
matically.

The early missionary endeavors in what is now Mexico reflect
the ambiguity of these ministerial efforts. On the one hand there
were those who sought to respect local culture and evangelize

within it, for example, Fray Pedro de Gante, noteworthy for presenting the Gospel within the indigenous idiom of song and drama. In several cases (Our Lady of Guadalupe is one) Christian sanctuaries were established on the sites of native peoples and in the manner of Fray de Gante the seeds of the Gospel were planted in the rituals, customs, practices, and fiestas of the people. On the other hand, the evangelization of Mexico was too often tainted by religious imperialism. Many missionaries condemned and suppressed as heretical all native religious practices and customs. Often they presented western culture and the Gospel as if the former was as divinely inspired as the latter.

Unfortunately these same patterns continued after the United States conquest of northern Mexico. Protestants said that Mexican-American Catholicism was pagan and superstitious; newly arrived French and Irish clergy claimed that the Catholicism of their co-religionists was superficial and lacking faith. Besides this frequent ridicule of Mexican-American religion, in many instances priests have forbidden use of the Spanish language for worship, even for baptisms, marriages, and funerals when a Spanish-speaking presider was available. Although church leaders have gradually become more open to the Mexican-American heritage of faith, many Mexican Americans and other Hispanics continue to sense that the official church considers their faith expressions inferior and unworthy.

Contemporary pastoral agents frequently serve Mexican-American and other communities whose faith expressions differ from their own. Part three examines liturgical ministry as a means of celebrating the sacred with these communities. The first essay offers the advice of a Mexican-American pastor to those who work with his people; the other two present the reflections of a pastoral agent who learned Spanish and some elements of Mexican-American history and religion as an adult. While immediately applicable to liturgical ministry with Mexican Americans and other Latinos, these essays also offer helpful insights for anyone who celebrates the sacred in communities with diverse worship traditions. In our experience, these communities provide a graced opportunity for pastoral agents to encounter Christ in a people's treasured expressions of faith.

5

The Treasure of Hispanic Faith

Virgilio P. Elizondo

THERE IS STILL A CERTAIN TENDENCY AMONG SOME PEOPLE TO LOOK UPON the Hispano as an unavoidable problem within the church and society. Some take a very negative view of the popular expressions of our Catholic faith that come out of our Latin American tradition and historical journey. Others, confusing acculturation with evangelization, want to Americanize us in the name of the Gospel.

There are those who would even say that we were never really evangelized and, therefore, were not really Christian. Those who still confuse unity with uniformity feel that by speaking Spanish and insisting on our traditions of faith—on the *sensus fidelium* of our particular church—we are being divisive.

Others feel that because we are concerned with the poor and rejected of society, we are mixing politics with spirituality and not giving sufficient attention to the work of the church. Many would be just as happy if we remained quietly buried in the tombs of poverty, illiteracy, and destitution and never came forth to disturb the structures of oppression and death.

The greatest difficulty of this type of problem-oriented mentality is precisely that people see only problems rather than God-given opportunities for growth, development, and new life. It blinds people from seeing the unique and privileged gift of God that the poor, the marginated, and the foreigner are to the church and society.

It is an undeniable first principle of Scripture and tradition that God chooses the absurd and the nothing of the world and commissions them to initiate new forms of life which will benefit the entire world.[1] Like the Jewish people of the Old Testament and the Galileans of the New, we Hispanics and the other minorities of the United States are not perfect or without sin. Yet precisely because we are often scorned and rejected by the powers of this world, we are called to become God's people and to assume the building of the new creation.

The wise and powerful of the world, and even of the church, seek reform and renewal only to discover themselves involved in destructive divisions. It is the simple and unsophisticated who are neither defending certain ways nor trying to force others in, but merely living out the life of God as it is interiorized in them by the Spirit. It is they who, without presuming to have anything to offer, will give to the church new and heretofore unsuspected insights which will transcend the dividing dichotomies and polemics of the present moment. It is the poor who will heal the wounds of the divisions that are damaging and threatening the life of the church.

Because of the way in which the world tends to look upon us, the greatest contribution that pastoral agents can make to the Hispanic communities is to have a fundamental change of attitude in relation to us. Do not see or fear us as an unsurmountable problem, but rejoice and appreciate us in our worldly lowliness as God's life-bearing gift, not only for the enrichment but even for the salvation of our church and our world.

If according to worldly wisdom we might appear to have nothing to offer except headaches and problems, let us as men and women of faith look to the tradition of our church for guidance and enlightenment. For it is there that we will discover the rich and unimagined potential of the United States Hispanic communities. Tradition is the life source of the church which anchors it firmly on Jesus Christ and guides it from within to its eschatological fulfillment.

Yet this tradition is not something static. It is the most dynamic element in the life and growth of the church. One of the most basic documents of Vatican II, the Dogmatic Constitution on Divine Revelation, clarifies how this tradition develops and guides the church forward toward the fullness of truth.

> This tradition which comes from the apostles develops in the church with the help of the Holy Spirit. For there is a growth in the understanding of the realities and the words which have been handed down. This happens through the contemplation and study made by believers, who treasure these things in their hearts (cf. Lk 2:19, 51) through the intimate understanding of spiritual things they experience, and through the preaching of those who have received through episcopal succession the sure gift of truth.[2]

The council does not state that the study and contemplation are to be made by scholars, bishops, or pastors alone, but clearly begins with the believers, that is, with the entire church. Furthermore, it does not send us primarily to books or ancient documents, but to those things which are treasured in the hearts of the believers as they were originally treasured in the heart of Mary, the first believer.

Let us not deceive ourselves. A faith that is portrayed as highly rational, intellectual, and complicated cannot be the good news to the simple and lowly of society for whom it is primarily intended. Faith is not only a new body of knowledge as such, but a new relationship which allows me to cry out from the innermost depths of my heart, Abba Father. From this new relationship, new knowledge, new values, new rites, new heroes, and new forms of life will certainly follow. But no amount of knowledge, moral rigidity, or liturgical precision can substitute for the Spirit who alone transforms the heart from within. The most basic tenet of the church is God's self-revelation as the loving and intimate Mother/Father who invites us to experience ourselves as beloved children.

On this point, the Hispanic church has much to contribute to the entire community of believers. The popular faith expressions are the most beloved treasure of our people. They are also concrete manifestations of the church's tradition as it has been interiorized in the hearts of the faithful by the Spirit. These expressions begin to accomplish the goal of evangelization as the transformation not only of human hearts and the various strata of society, but even culture itself. Hence it should not be surprising that Paul VI told the Hispanic Catholics of the United States that we should not put aside our legitimate religious practices, nor that he told the entire world that popular piety manifests a thirst for God which only the simple and the poor can know.[3]

If you will listen to our prayer forms, take part in our processions, devotions, and liturgical fiestas, listen to our ordinary first names, and see the decorations in our neighborhoods, homes, and even on our bodies, you will quickly discover that faith for us is not an abstract formula or merely a Sunday affair, but the fundamental living reality of our lives. In our devotion to the saints, the doctrines of our church are personalized and become human stories.

We meet *Papacito Dios* (Daddy God) from the earliest days of our lives and God remains a constant source of support throughout life. We communicate easily and in a very personal way with God as Father, with Mary as our mother, with Jesus as our Lord and brother, and with the saints and souls in purgatory as members of our extended family. We argue with them, we ask them favors, we tell them jokes, we include them in our popular songs, we visit and converse easily with them.[4] We keep pictures or images of them alongside the portraits of the family and best friends. We do not consider them graven images but rather simple expressions of our dearest friends. Their friendship is one of our deepest treasures and has enabled us to withstand the rejection of society without deep scars and to endure the suffering of oppression without giving up hope.

Yet our intimacy with them cannot be reduced to an opium which will drug us so as to keep us oppressed. The banner of Our Lady of Guadalupe has led all our struggles for justice—from the first struggles for independence to the present day movements of the farm workers. She has been our leader and our strength. Mary has been our banner, the rosary has been our marching cadence, and the religious songs have been our invincible spirit.

Like Mary, we treasure in our hearts the revelations of Jesus as we have experienced him in the annual reenactment of the journey to Bethlehem in the *posadas*, the birth of Jesus, the visit of the shepherds and later on of the astrologers, the day of earth on Ash Wednesday, the *Semana Santa* (Holy Week) with the procession of palms, the washing of feet, the agony in the garden, the passion and death of Jesus, the *siete palabras* (seven last words), his burial and the *pésame* (condolences) to his mother, the *Sabado de Gloria* (Saturday of Glory) with the dramatic reenactment of the resurrection, May, the month of Mary, June of the Sacred Heart and Corpus Christi, October of the rosary, November of the communion of saints, all culminating with the great feast of Christ the King.[5]

The first missioners, who planted the seeds of our *sensus fidelium*, were aware of the need to experience the fundamental elements of the mystery of Christ in a living way. For experience of Christ is the beginning of faith.

In these experiences of the historical events upon which the Creed is based, the people spontaneously intuit much of Christianity's deepest meaning. They may not be able to express it through the doctrinal formulation or theological discourse of the educated elite, but as you hear them speaking about what it means to them in their lives, as many of us experienced in the Cursillo movement, there is certainly no doubt whatsoever that they truly intuit the deepest meaning of our faith.[6]

These living experiences give us a simple and very enjoyable way of not just hearing explanations about the mystery of Christ, but actually living them out. Sermons and catechetical classes we forget easily, but those things that we have experienced together with the other believers and have deeply marked our minds and hearts will never be forgotten.

This type of evangelization and catechesis has great advantages:

1. These celebrations and devotions are easily accessible not just to a few but to the masses of the people. It is through these practices that the church can best fulfill her mandate of universality and truly reach the hearts of the masses.[7]

2. They are enjoyed by all and in various ways they touch everyone—from the youngest to the oldest, from the frivolous to the pious, from the sober to the drunk, from the intellectuals to the illiterate, from the mystics to the unbelievers. No one is left untouched when he or she has participated in one of these reenactments of Christ's life. Through these celebrations the faithful come to appreciate the spiritual signification of the things that they experience together.

3. Because we take part in them from birth, they become the core symbols of our life and the deepest treasures of our heart. Some among the community will conceptualize and investigate the explicit meaning and message to these mysteries and their full implications in daily life, but even for those who cannot explain them rationally, they will still be of ultimate and transcendental signification.

Where these expressions of the Catholic faith are missing from the churches, the Hispanics will likewise be missing. They will seek them out wherever they are being celebrated and celebrate them on their own if they cannot be found. They are our way of incarnating and making fully alive the presence of Jesus, his way, and his church.

In all the beauty of our tradition there was one element missing that we are quickly discovering with great joy: direct contact with the Scriptures. Once introduced to it, Hispanics have a great love for the Bible and enjoy discussing it and studying it seriously. It is the study and celebration of the Scriptures that is bringing out the deeper meaning which is encased in the various expressions of our tradition.

The renewal of Vatican II has emphasized the question of meaning, but the tragedy is that much of the western church often continues to reduce meaning to conceptual and verbal knowledge, and thus to lose sight of that knowledge of the heart which human reason itself cannot understand. This is not because it is irrational, but because it is transrational!

Advertisers certainly know this well, for in order to sell products they appeal to the inner yearnings of the heart and not to rational discourse. Let me state it clearly. We are not in any way denying the need for serious intellectual study, but we are stating that no amount of knowledge alone can replace or substitute for the treasures of the heart, for it is in the hearts of the faithful that the Spirit dwells as in a temple.[8] It is from the treasures of the heart that study and contemplation must begin.

But these expressions are not mere externals. They reflect a life of deep faith not just in God but in the kingdom of God, which means God's way for humanity. They are both the signs of the way of life and the ongoing sources for this way of life.

Among the Hispanic poor people, there are many living gospel values which are expressed through our culture that I hope will not die out as we enter into a highly individualistic and technological society. The strong emphasis is on the extended family and family values, a Christian sense of suffering with resignation and hope, spontaneous hospitality and generosity, our humor and way of life, a deep and unquestioned sense of the providence of God, a warm and personal sense of faith, and respect and love of children and old people, who are the kings and queens of the home.

There is an entire way of life that is embodied and expressed in our religious symbols. Since life and symbol are intimately linked one to another, as one disappears so will the other.

Today our popular expressions of the faith should not be merely tolerated or, even worse, ridiculed. Rather, they should be joyously welcomed into the total life of the United States church. The religious treasures we carry in our hearts are the greatest gift that we bring to the life of the church in this country.

Catholics in our country are hungry for visible expressions of our Catholic heritage. They are tired of the polarizations of the left and the right. Incorporating the faith expressions of the poor and the marginated into the life of the church will be not only a powerful source of unity, but also a clear witness that the Gospel is being lived and proclaimed in fidelity to the way of Jesus and the church.

> But Christ also carried out this proclamation by innumerable signs . . . and among all these signs there is the one to which he attaches great importance: the humble and the poor are evangelized, become his disciples and gather together "in his name" in the great community of these who believe in him.[9]

Yet as positive a picture as I have painted, I am well aware that within our Hispanic community there is likewise imperfection, corruption, sin, and the need for growth and development. This is why we need the fellowship of the entire church. We need bishops with their theologians, priests, catechists, and other ministers who will share the same treasures of the heart which come through the intimate understanding of the spiritual things we experience together.

Preaching and teaching must arise out of the living reality of the faith, which is always historically and culturally conditioned.[10] Otherwise, it will come across more as foreign imposition or a sort of religious ideology which will destroy people more than lead them to perfection. Thus we need pastoral agents who will not seek to put us down in the name of the Gospel but who will treasure the same culturally conditioned expressions of the faith, and in the light of Scripture and tradition purify and ennoble them so that they will more clearly express the glory of God.

The task of the Gospel is never to destroy but to enrich, liberate, and perfect. Pastoral agents are to be one in heart with the

Christian community in whose fellowship you share so that out of that living experience you can grow in faith with that community. If you truly appreciate the spiritual experiences of the people, then you will be prepared to carry out the traditional manner of teaching in the church—mystagogical catechesis—through which the meaning and implications of the mysteries that have already been experienced are explained and illuminated in the light of our Catholic faith. Out of the common experience, we need pastoral agents to develop with us and sometimes even for us the full meaning of our faith.

Notes

1. 1 Cor 1:27-31; Mk 10:17ff; Mt 19:16ff; Lk 18:18ff; Mk 14:5ff; Mt 5:3; Lk 6:20 and 16:19. See also John Paul II, Homily in the Barrio of Santa Cecilia, 30 January 1979; The Conclusions of the Third General Conference of Latin American Bishops (Puebla) 1134-1165; Paul VI, apostolic exhortation *Evangelii Nuntiandi*; Virgilio Elizondo, *Galilean Journey: The Mexican-American Promise* (Maryknoll, N.Y.: Orbis, 1983) especially chapters 4 and 7.

2. Vatican Council II: Dogmatic Constitution on Divine Revelation 8.

3. *Evangelii Nuntiandi* 20, 48; Paul VI, Radio Message to the Hispanic People, 18 August 1977. It is likewise interesting to note that popular religion has become an important *locus theologicus* for U.S. Latino theology.

4. For an example of such intimacy with God, Mary, and the saints, see the conversations of Doña Margarita in Victor Villaseñor, *Rain of Gold* (Houston: Arte Publico, 1991) 423-425, 474-475.

5. For further clarification and elaboration, see the first two essays in this collection.

6. John Paul II, Address to Latin American Bishops at Puebla, 28 January 1979.

7. *Evangelii Nuntiandi* 57; Conclusions of the Third General Conference of Latin American Bishops (Puebla) 449.

8. 1 Cor 3:16, 6:19; Vatican II: Dogmatic Constitution on the Church 4.

9. *Evangelii Nuntiandi* 12.

10. John Paul II's address to the Pontifical Biblical Commission, 26 April 1979, has some excellent insights on this point.

6

Liturgy, Popular Rites, and Popular Spirituality

Timothy M. Matovina

BERNARD LONERGAN EXPLAINS THE HORIZON OF THE HUMAN SUBJECT BY comparing it to the literal meaning of horizon. He notes that in the physical world, horizon is the limit of what the eye can see, the boundary within which objects can be seen and beyond which, at least for the moment, objects cannot be seen. So too with the human subject, the horizon is the limit of what the subject can see or imagine, the boundary within which lie our knowledge and our interests, and beyond which lie questions and interests which we have not yet even imagined to ask or to consider.[1]

Margaret Mary Kelleher has applied Lonergan's notion of horizon to the liturgical assembly, finding that in its ritual praxis as collective subject a public horizon is mediated, that is, "the limit of the assembly's imagination." She calls on liturgical theology to take on the task of scrutinizing these horizons, asking questions about the ritual subject or assembly, the ritual symbols, and the ritual process. This task is a process of observing the liturgical praxis of a given assembly, interpreting that praxis in order to objectify its public horizon, judging its authenticity against the message of Christ, and acting for the promotion of change.[2]

In this chapter I will use Kelleher's methodology to scrutinize the public horizon of the *posada* as celebrated among Mexican-American communities. This attempt to objectify the public

81

horizon of the *posada* will include an examination of the *posada* rite itself, the performance of the rite, and the place of the *posada* within the whole ritual field of Mexican-American popular rites. From this analysis I will postulate some conclusions on the study of the public horizon of popular rites as a resource for the celebration of the sacraments, especially Sunday eucharist.

It needs to be noted that I am assuming popular rites are part of Catholicism and not some unwanted but persistent stepchild. There is continued discussion on what the official church should do to curtail or control popular religious rites, but the simple fact is these rites mediate their community's public horizon and will continue to do so. Segundo Galilea argues that the common term "popular religiosity" should be replaced with the theologically richer "popular spirituality" where spirituality means "the practices and attitudes which express the experience of God in a person, a culture, a Christian community."[3] I concur with his thesis and will use his terminology as well as "popular rites" in place of the pejorative "popular folk practices." In my view, the primary theological question is not what to do about popular religious rites but how to articulate and objectify the spirituality, horizon, and subsequent Christology, ecclesiology, and meaning of discipleship which these rites express. Such articulation enables us to place them in dialogue with the horizon mediated in "official" rites and thus engage in a mutual critique.

LA POSADA

The *posada* (literally "dwelling" or "shelter") focuses on the pilgrims Mary and Joseph on their way to Bethlehem. In this novena celebration (16-24 December) the participants reenact this historical pilgrimage in a candlelight procession, carrying statues of Joseph, Mary, and the donkey to various houses and asking *posada* for the evening. After a series of rejections they gain entry and hospitality at the final home. Each night a different home is chosen to have the honor of receiving the pilgrims. The offering of *posada* to the pilgrims is followed by a fiesta which celebrates the joy of their being accepted. One of the highlights of the fiesta is the *piñata*, a brightly decorated container filled with candy and other surprises which blindfolded children take turns trying to break open with a stick.

The *posada* has its origins in the early Spanish missionary efforts in the New World. It combines the devotional impulse of Iberian Catholicism and the impulse for dramatic ritual, pantomime in storytelling, and fiesta of the indigenous peoples of what is now Mexico. The central text of the rite is an ancient pilgrimage song. After knocking at the door of the house, the participants sing this song antiphonally. The group outside the house represents the voice of the pilgrims and the group inside represents the owners of the *posada*, as follows:

AFUERA:
En nombre del cielo
os pido posada
pues no puede andar
mi esposa amada.

OUTSIDE:
In the name of heaven
I ask you for lodging
because to keep on going
my beloved wife is unable.

ADENTRO:
Aquí no es mesón,
Sigan adelante,
y no puedo abrir,
no sea algun tunante.

INSIDE:
This is not an inn;
continue on your way;
I can't open [the door];
you may be riffraff.

AFUERA:
No seas inhumano,
Ténnos caridad,
que el Dios de los cielos
te lo premiará.

OUTSIDE:
Don't be inhuman;
have charity for us
that the God of heaven
may repay you for it.

ADENTRO:
Ya se pueden ir
y no molestar,
porque si me enfado
os voy a apalear.

INSIDE:
You may go now
and don't bother us,
because if I get angry
I'm going to hit you.

AFUERA:
Venimos rendidos
desde Nazaret.
Yo soy carpintero
de nombre José.

OUTSIDE:
We are very tired,
coming from Nazareth.
I am a carpenter,
Joseph by name.

ADENTRO:
No me importa el nombre,
déjenme dormir,
pues que ya les digo
que no hemos de abrir.

INSIDE:
I don't care about your name;
let me sleep;
I already told you
that we're not going to open.

After these verses are sung at the houses where the pilgrims are rejected, the following verses are added at the last house where they are received:

AFUERA:
Posada te pide,
amado casero,
por solo una noche
la Reina del Cielo.

OUTSIDE:
Asking you for lodging,
kind homeowner,
for only one night,
is the Queen of Heaven.

ADENTRO:
Pues si es una reina
quien lo solicita,
¿como es que de noche
anda tan solita?

INSIDE:
If she is a queen
who is asking,
how is it that at night
she is walking alone?

AFUERA:
Mi esposa es María,
es reina del Cielo,
y madre va a ser
del Divino Verbo.

OUTSIDE:
My wife is Mary,
she is the Queen of Heaven,
and she is going to be mother
of the Divine Word.

ADENTRO:
¿Eres tu José?
¿Tu esposa es María?
Entren peregrinos,
no los conocía.

INSIDE:
Are you Joseph?
Your wife is Mary?
Come in, pilgrims,
I did not know who you were.

AFUERA:
Dios pague, señores,
vuestra caridad
y así os colme el cielo
de felicidad.

OUTSIDE:
May God reward, good persons,
your charity,
and may heaven fill you
with happiness.

ADENTRO:
¡Dichosa la casa
que abriga este día
a la Virgen pura,
la hermosa María!

INSIDE:
Happy the home
that houses today
the pure Virgin,
the beautiful Mary!

TODOS, MIENTRAS
LOS PEREGRINOS ENTRAN:
Entren santos peregrinos,
reciban este rincón
no de esta pobre morada
sino de mi corazón.

ALL, AS PILGRIMS ENTER:

Come in, holy pilgrims,
accept this corner,
not of this poor house,
but of my heart.

Esta noche es de alegría,	This is a night of happiness,
de gusto y de regocijo,	of joy and rejoicing,
porque hospedamos aquí	because we give hospitality here
a la Madre de Dios Hijo.	to the Mother of God the Son.[4]

THE RITE ITSELF

The words, gestures, and symbols of the *posada* celebration suggest aspects of its horizon of meaning that have been articulated by Mexican-American theologians. Virgilio Elizondo has described three such meanings. One is that the rejected are recognized as God's chosen ones, that what this world ignores or discards God esteems as of great value. Another is the joy of hospitality for those who accept the rejected pilgrims. It is not the pilgrims but those who own the house of *posada* who lead the celebration and the joy, as is indicated in the last four stanzas of the pilgrim song. Thirdly, the *posada* embodies the theme of "following the way," of walking with the holy pilgrims through the darkness of rejection to the light, warmth, and joy of being received that comes to those who persevere on the way.[5]

Angela Erevia offers three other aspects of the *posada's* horizon. She sees in the novena aspect of the *posada* an Advent theme of waiting for the coming of Christ. In some communities the rite is supplemented with a progression of scripture readings which augment this aspect of the nine *posadas*. Second, the *posada* celebrates the incarnation of Christ in us, offering the holy pilgrims not just a corner "of this poor house" but also the *corazón* (heart) of the participants that Christ might be born into the world again through them. Finally, like many popular religious rites, the *posada* celebrates the Christianization of our environment, that is, the presence of the sacred in the homes and everyday lives of the people. God and religion are not something out there but are very close; the sacred rite of the holy pilgrims is a visible reminder that the saints, the divine, and the sacred are continually present in the life of the *barrio* (neighborhood).[6]

The above is by no means an exhaustive list of the *posada's* themes, but a summary of the insights from two Mexican-American pastoral theologians who have experienced and studied the rite. Their reflections reveal that the *posada* rite itself shapes the horizon of the participants: it can help them to see beyond present rejection, persevere in the way despite hardships, wait in the spirit of Advent for the coming of Christ, see their hearts and lives as the place where Christ is to be born, and recall the presence of the sacred in their environment, calling them to Christianize it.

PERFORMANCE OF THE RITE

As with any liturgy, the horizon of the *posada* is mediated only in the way that it is celebrated in a given community. A *posada* that is merely an excuse for a fiesta will not carry all the rich meanings outlined above. A *posada* that is clerically dominated or dominated by a single person or small group of persons against the community's consent will present a different kind of horizon by its very praxis. A *posada* that is manipulated into an instrument of proselytizing in order to increase membership in a parish or prayer group will present a horizon more tied up with particular interests than the horizon of the rite itself. In other words, every family and community that celebrates the *posada* mediates a horizon of meaning based on the rite that is used but also on their praxis in the celebration of that rite.

I will offer two reflections by way of example on the horizon of the celebration of the *posada* from six years experience I had with the Hispanic community at Holy Family parish in Missouri City, Texas. The first concerns community leadership. Many of the leaders who initiated the *posadas* in their family or neighborhood, or who became prayer leaders and organizers, were persons who for reasons of discrimination, lack of self-confidence, or lack of an invitation never had taken on a role of leadership in the parish, its religious societies, or other community organizations. In the *posada* celebrations they found a worship community in which leadership was based on charism rather than ascribed status, on knowledge of their own culture rather than the dominant culture, on popular spirituality rather than liturgical spirituality, on creating an ambience of warmth and welcome rather than executing a rite precisely. A selection process for leadership which was more inclusive and more attentive to these values of the local culture is one aspect of the actual celebration of the *posada* rite which mediated a collective horizon to us as a community.

My second reflection is the way this rite was interpreted as calling the parish to receive the immigrants arriving in our midst. It was a common practice to invite newcomers to receive a *posada* into their homes as a way of welcoming them. Parish volunteers who had worked to help immigrants apply for amnesty were honored at a festive *posada* which connected the hospitality extended in working with amnesty to the hospitality shown Mary and Joseph. These ways of celebrating the *posada* mediated the meaning that to celebrate the rite authentically the community had to offer *posada* to Mary and Joseph present in the immigrant community today.

In this particular community the way in which the *posada* was celebrated set a standard for who could assume community leadership and how the local community should respond to arriving immigrants. These are just two examples of how in large part the performance of the *posada* rite, for better and for worse, determines the horizon of meaning it mediates to the collective imagination of a particular community.

ETHNIC IDENTIFICATION

The *posada* cannot be understood in isolation. It must be understood within the wider context of the whole ritual field of rites that Mexican-American popular spirituality encompasses. When seen in this context, a further aspect of the horizon mediated by the *posada* (and Mexican-American popular rites as a whole) can be seen: that of ethnic identification.

Harry S. Stout has hypothesized that most religions in the United States follow a similar three stage development. The first stage is that of immigrant religion in which ethnic and religious identity are inextricably bound, for example, in the life of the Puritans; German, Irish, Italian and other Catholic immigrant groups; German Lutherans; and Black Americans (although the latter were not immigrants in most cases). The second stage is the breaking down of the immigrant religions into Protestant-Catholic-Jewish-Black ethnoreligions. At this stage the process of assimilation breaks down the ties to the cultural group and identity is more linked to a larger ethnic norm in a particular religious denomination. For example, Lutherans of German ancestry identify themselves less as "German" and more as

"Lutheran" or simply "Protestant." The final stage is civil religion where the real religion becomes the American way of life itself, characterized by individual pragmatism, materialism, faith in progress through technology, and nationalism. At this final stage assimilation into these four cultural values is so complete that ethnic identity and denomination have little (if any) further significance.[7]

There are many aspects of Stout's thesis which merit discussion, but what is of interest here is his contention that most religions in the United States begin as immigrant religions whose immigrant character later dissolves due to assimilation and the breakdown of ethnic identity. This has certainly been true of United States Catholicism which was in the nineteenth century predominately a church of national ethnic parishes. In this first stage of mass Catholicism in America the major ethnic groups held tenaciously to their particular brands of cultural Catholicism. The Germans thoroughly transplanted their brand of Catholicism in their national parishes, bringing with them German nativity scenes and statues, the custom of an elaborately decorated empty tomb for Easter, their great love for music and colorful public processions, eucharistic devotions, and the tradition of numerous parish *vereins* or confraternities and societies. Irish Catholics refused to cease their festive funerals with elaborate processions and wakes despite ecclesiastical pressure to do so. The Italians had the strongest devotion to their own popular rites, particularly the *festa* or celebration of the saint or madonna after which a particular village in Italy was named. Italian observance of the *festa* was too deeply ingrained in their culture to be eradicated even by the frequent protests of the Catholic hierarchy and the condemnation of their Protestant neighbors. Despite this extreme attachment to immigrant Catholicism among the Germans, Irish, Italians, and others in the nineteenth century, however, today the national parish and cultural Catholicism among these groups have been considerably weakened and in many places totally eliminated. This is due in large part not to ecclesiastical pressure, but to the assimilation of many Catholics from the poor and working classes to the middle class in the post-World War II era. The shift from greater ethnic identity to a more homogenized denominational identity as many Catholics have entered the middle class and become more "Americanized" is what one would expect if Stout's thesis is indeed true.[8]

For a variety of reasons, however, this thesis does not appear to be true of many Mexican Americans and other Hispanics. It is true that many individuals have assimilated into the mainstream of American life, culture, and values, but as a whole there has been great resistance to assimilation. While the reasons for this are much too complex to examine adequately here, we could consider the greater proximity to their countries of origin, the continuous flow of new immigrants, the fact that many Mexican Americans did not immigrate at all but were conquered, and the persistent poverty of those who cannot or do not want to "ascend" to the middle class.[9]

The import of all this for our study is that to resist the powerful dynamic of assimilation (for whatever reason) an equally powerful dynamic of religious rites and symbols is needed. Ricardo Ramirez claims that popular religion serves this function as "a defense and protest against the demands of the dominant culture." Elizondo concurs with this insight:

> The conquest of ancient Mexico by Spain in 1521 and then the conquest of northern Mexico by the United States in the 1840s forced the native population and their succeeding generations into a split and meaningless existence. It was a mortal collective catastrophe of gigantic death-bearing consequences. Yet the people have survived as a people through the emergence of new religious symbols and the reinterpretation of old ones which have connected the past with the present and projected into the future.[10]

Another aspect of the horizon mediated by the *posada*, then, along with other rites of Mexican-American popular spirituality, is the reinforcement of ethnic identity. Like the Irish, Germans, Italians, and other Catholics before them, Mexican Americans find in their popular rites an orientation toward life in an often hostile, unfamiliar, and unintelligible environment. The *posada* reassures its participants that they do have an identity as a people and that their group symbols, customs, and approach to life, even if not acceptable in the world of the dominant culture, are of value in the world of the holy pilgrims.

PASTORAL IMPLICATIONS

The Constitution on the Sacred Liturgy called for the critique of popular devotions using official liturgy as a norm. I suggest that this critique should be a mutual one: liturgy also needs to be critiqued by popular rites and the horizon they mediate.[11] This is true not only of Mexican-American communities, but in the popular rites of local communities in general. The horizon of popular rites illuminates some of the meanings the local community seeks to celebrate in liturgy. In the case of the *posada* for the Mexican-American community these include the joy of accepting the rejected, inspiration to persevere in the way despite hardship, a call to Christianize our environment, a more inclusive selection process for leaders which is attentive to local cultural values, hospitality to immigrants and newcomers, and reinforcement of ethnic identity (acceptance as a people) in an often hostile environment.

It is well within the range of the eucharist (and other sacramental celebrations) to embody much of this range of meaning, if we are willing to discern the horizon which the *posadas* and other popular rites present and incorporate it into our Sunday worship. For example, in communities where the *posada* tradition is practiced, the fourth Sunday of Advent provides a good opportunity to incorporate a modified celebration of that tradition into the eucharist.[12] By including those who lead neighborhood or home *posadas* in the preparation and celebration of that Sunday's eucharist, the *posada* and the eucharist can mutually enrich one another. Practitioners of the *posada* can offer the community the dramatic proclamation of the hospitality offered the pilgrims Mary and Joseph, calling those present to offer *posada* in their lives that Christ might be welcomed and born anew. Those charged with ministering at eucharist can animate the assembly in this Sunday's celebration to integrate the rich meanings of the *posada* with those of the Advent season. The gospel selections for that Sunday are on Mary's role in the incarnation and are conducive to the theme of making *posada* for Christ in our lives, in our families, in our communities, and in our world. Perhaps it could be stated that the most intimate way we offer *posada* is in the eucharist, receiving Christ in the word, in communion, and in one another. In these ways our liturgy will be enriched while the *posada* and other popular rites will be more deeply enriched by the sacramental life of the church.

Notes

1. Bernard Lonergan, *Method in Theology* (New York: Herder and Herder, 1972) 235-236.
2. Margaret Mary Kelleher, "Liturgical Theology: A Task and a Method," *Worship* 62 (January 1988) 2-24.
3. Segundo Galilea, *Religiosidad popular y pastoral Hispano-Americana* (New York: Northeast Catholic Pastoral Center for Hispanics, 1981) 49. Quotation is author's translation of text.
4. Virgilio Elizondo, *Galilean Journey: The Mexican-American Promise* (Maryknoll, N.Y.: Orbis, 1983) 36-37.
5. Ibid. 34-38. This material is on pages 7-12 above.
6. Angela Erevia, *Possibilities for Catechetics and Liturgy for the Mexican American Community* (San Antonio: Mexican American Cultural Center Press, 1974) 38.
7. Harry Stout, "Ethnicity: The Vital Center for Religion in America," *Ethnicity* 2 (1975) 204-224.
8. Jay Dolan, *The Immigrant Church* (Notre Dame: University of Notre Dame Press, 1983) 60-62, 76-81; Robert Vecoli, "Italian Immigrants and the Catholic Church," *Journal of Social History* 2 (1969) 228, 231-235; Robert Orsi, *The Madonna of 115th St.: Faith and Community in Italian Harlem, 1880-1950* (New Haven: Yale University Press, 1986); Dean Hoge, "Interpreting Change in American Catholicism: The River and the Floodgate," *Review* of *Religious Research* 27 (June 1986) 292-294.
9. Timothy M. Matovina, "Hispanic Catholics in the United States: No Melting Pot in Sight," *America* 164 (16 March 1991) 289-290.
10. Ricardo Ramirez, "Liturgy from the Mexican American Perspective," *Worship* 51 (July 1977) 296; Virgilio Elizondo, "Popular Religion as Support of Identity; A Pastoral-Psychological Case-Study Based on the Mexican American Experience in the USA," in *Popular Religion,* ed. Norbert Greinacher and Norbert Mette (Edinburg: T. & T. Clark, 1986) 42-43. The latter reference is the second essay in this collection.
11. *Sacrosanctum Concilium* 13; conclusions from the Third General Conference of Latin American Bishops (Puebla) 465; Anscar J. Chupungco, *Liturgical Inculturation: Sacramentals, Religiosity, and Catechesis* (Collegeville: The Liturgical Press, 1992) especially chapter three "Popular Religiosity and Liturgical Inculturation," 95-133.
12. Arturo Pérez has suggested that the *posadas* can also be incorporated into the entrance rites on Christmas Eve. Arturo Pérez, *Popular Catholicism: A Hispanic Perspective* (Washington, D.C.: Pastoral Press 1988) 21.

7

Marriage Celebrations in Mexican-American Communities

Timothy M. Matovina

THE 1969 REVISED RITE OF MARRIAGE AND THE CURRENT REVISED DRAFT provide more flexibility for celebrating marriage than the official rites for any other sacrament. This flexibility has allowed episcopal conferences in nations such as Germany, France, and Ireland to adapt the marriage ritual for use in their countries. In 1983 the Holy See approved the Tagalog Rite proposed by church leaders from the Philippines. This alternative rite integrates the Roman ritual with local marriage customs, creating a nuptial liturgy based both on Roman Catholic tradition and the cultural genius of the Filipino people.[1]

In the United States, the Bishops' Committee for Pastoral Research and Practice commented on local practices for the celebration of marriage with their 1990 publication *Planning Your Wedding Ceremony*.[2] The bishops' committee recognizes that various additions and alterations to the prescribed wedding liturgy, although "not officially approved," are gaining wider usage among U.S. faith communities. For example, wedding liturgies in the United States occasionally feature a symbolic offering for the poor given during the presentation of the gifts; this offering represents the couple's desire to serve the needy as part of the marital covenant. Another addition to the rite is a brief commentary that parents or invited guests give to the couple after the postcommunion prayer or, when marriage is celebrated outside of

Mass, before the final blessing. Similar to the prepared remarks sometimes offered at funeral liturgies, this commentary is particularly prevalent at African-American and Vietnamese wedding ceremonies. In some U.S. parishes the entrance procession is altered from the common form of the bride escorted by her father (a practice not actually prescribed in the Roman rite), allowing instead for the bride's mother and father to accompany her, or for both the bride and groom to process in with their parents. This increasingly popular adaptation expresses the couple's origin from both sets of parents and eliminates the ritual "handing over" of the bride as if she were property.

The bishops' committee also mentions four faith expressions frequently used at Mexican-American weddings: the *arras* (thirteen gold or silver coins), *lazo* (a figure-eight band, often comprised of two rosaries), bouquet to the Blessed Virgin Mary, and parental blessing of the couple. Other elements of Mexican-American marriage rites include the *padrinos* (godparents), the *cojines* (cushions), the *libro y rosario* (prayer book or Bible and rosary), and the *velo* (veil).

This chapter will describe a typical order of service for Mexican-American marriage celebrations, outline the historical development of these rites, summarize some contemporary interpretations of Mexican-American marriage traditions, and offer guidelines for liturgists and other pastoral agents who prepare and celebrate this sacrament with Mexican-American communities.

DESCRIPTION

Mexican-American families consistently promote the inclusion of *padrinos* in sacramental rites. Godparents are chosen not just for baptism and confirmation but also for First Communion, the maturing to adulthood of a young woman *(quinceañera)*, and marriage. The significance of *padrinos* for Mexican Americans is also evident in the concern that they occupy a prominent place in the liturgy. This ritual inclusion forms a spiritual bond between the *padrinos* and the families of the couple, a bond that is reinforced in a fiesta continuing the sacramental celebration, a fiesta for which the *padrinos* provide financial and other support.[3]

Padrinos usually participate in the entrance procession as couples, each couple bearing the gift that they have "sponsored" for the celebration: the *cojines,* the *arras,* the *libro y rosario,* the bouquet, the *lazo.* All proceed to their assigned places, except the *padrinos* of the *cojines,* who first place the cushions on the kneeler used by the bride and groom and then join the other *padrinos.* In addition to the sponsors who bear gifts, the *primer padrinos* (first godparents, sometimes called *padrinos de iglesia* or *padrinos de velación*) take part in the entrance procession. The *primer padrinos* sponsor the newlyweds for the sacrament of marriage in the same way that godparents sponsor a baptized child (or adult) in the faith. Because of their preeminence, they usually enter just before the bride (and groom, if he processes) and are seated in a place of particular prominence, oftentimes near the couple in the sanctuary. The *padrinos,* who normally are at least a generation older than the couple, are frequently complemented by a bridal party (*chambelanes* and *damas*) of the couple's contemporaries, although some Mexican-American families invite only one of the two groups.

After the greeting and the Liturgy of the Word, the *primer padrinos* come forward to function as the primary witnesses; they stand near the couple or in some other suitable place. Following the statement of intentions and the exchange of vows and rings, the priest or deacon calls forth the other *padrinos* and blesses the various gifts they present, either individually or collectively. Then the *padrinos* offer their gifts. *Padrinos* who sponsor the *arras* give them to the groom, who in turn presents them to the bride. The Mexican Sacramentary offers the following invocation for the presentation of the *arras:*

> Groom:
> Receive these coins; they are a pledge of the care I will take so that we won't lack what is necessary in our home.
>
> Bride:
> I receive them as a sign of the care I will take so that our home will prosper.[4]

Next the *padrinos* of the *libro y rosario,* followed by the *padrinos* of the bouquet, present their gifts to the bride. Finally the couple kneels and the last set of *padrinos* unite the newlyweds with the *lazo.* Sometimes the hem of the bride's *velo* is placed over the shoulder of the groom, where the *lazo* holds it in place; apparently this practice is a residue from an earlier rite in which bride and groom were "veiled" as one after the exchange of vows. In many parishes the priest or deacon comments on the significance of the *libro y rosario*, bouquet, and *lazo* as they are presented, formulating their own invocations since the official rites contain no instructions or suggested prayer texts for practices other than the *arras*. When all of these rites are concluded, the liturgy continues with the general intercessions.

The *padrinos* of the *lazo* later remove it, usually after the nuptial blessing. Before the final blessing the bride offers the bouquet, along with a prayer of dedication and intercession, before a figure of Our Lady of Guadalupe or some other Marian image. Although sometimes celebrated in the home rather than the church, the parental blessing of the couple is frequently offered at the time of the final blessing in the wedding liturgy. Alternatively, the parents simply place their hands on the couple in silence as the deacon or priest pronounces the nuptial blessing.

Since most of these faith expressions are not prescribed in the official rites, it is not surprising that they differ from parish to parish and even from family to family. The marriage ritual described here reflects the general pattern of Mexican-American worship, but pastoral ministers encounter numerous variations on this schema. These variations include the order of service, the texts (if any) that accompany specific actions and gifts, and the omission of some practices (e.g., a couple will have *arras* and *lazo* but no *libro y rosario*).

HISTORICAL BACKGROUND

Although a comprehensive history of Mexican-American marriage rites is beyond the scope of this work, an overview of this history provides valuable insights for pastoral agents and others who celebrate marriage with Mexican-American communities. For example, the development of marriage rites on the Iberian peninsula reflects the contemporary Mexican-American penchant for incorporating popular customs into the liturgy. The influence of Roman colonization began on the peninsula before the Christian era and lasted for nearly four centuries. Invaders from the north arrived early in the fifth century, including the Visigoths who settled alongside the Christians. The Goths converted to Christianity in 589 and blended their traditions with those of their predecessors. Thus local marriage rites included practices like uniting the couple together with a cord, which was probably Visigothic, along with the Roman veiling of the bride. Isidore, the early seventh-century archbishop of Seville, promoted these expressions, interpreting the cord as a reminder that spouses "should in no way disrupt the compact of marital unity" and the veil as a sign that women are to be humble, modest, and "subject to their husbands." Later liturgical books document the incorporation of the Visigothic custom of the *arras* (literally, "pledges") into the liturgy. Originally a betrothal pledge given to the woman's family, by the eleventh century the *arras* had been incorporated into the marriage liturgy as a mutual exchange of marital pledge gifts, usually in the form of two rings.[5]

With some variations and adaptations, including the presentation of coins as a symbolic marital pledge *(arras)* along with the exchange of rings, these rites persisted on the Iberian peninsula and were prevalent during the sixteenth-century Spanish colonization of the indigenous peoples in Mexico. Early missioners to Mexico were far more concerned with polygamy among the native population than they were with fostering local marriage rites. Nonetheless, at least two Aztec marriage customs reflect elements of Spanish Catholic nuptial rituals. When an Aztec couple wed, they sat on separate mats, which were then joined by tassels to signify their marital union. In addition, the groom's family bestowed gifts on the bride.[6]

These practices mirror the Visigothic traditions of joining the couple by a *lazo* and the groom presenting a marital pledge or *arras*. While the extent of indigenous influence on contemporary marriage traditions among Mexicans and Mexican-Americans is unclear, these Aztec customs could easily have affected both native reception of Spanish Catholic rites and the missionaries' performance of those rites among the peoples they sought to evangelize.

Long-standing marital customs continued among people of Mexican heritage who were incorporated into the United States after the U.S. conquest of northern Mexico in the mid-nineteenth century. Foreign clergy assigned to the conquered territories encountered traditions like the *arras* and *velo*, which their congregants taught them to celebrate.[7] The widespread practice of

Mexican-American marriage traditions in today's parishes demonstrates their enduring significance. At the same time, contemporary interpretations and pastoral adaptations reflect the ongoing evolution of these rites.

CONTEMPORARY INTERPRETATIONS

Theologians, pastoral ministers, and practitioners of Mexican-American faith expressions have articulated interpretations of marital customs prevalent in Mexican-American communities. Although liturgists and other pastoral agents will find some of these commentaries more helpful than others, recognizing the range of extant interpretations provides valuable insights about the worshipers that liturgical ministers serve.

Traditions like the parental blessing require no detailed exegesis, of course. However, gifts that appear to have a purely utilitarian purpose, such as the *cojines*, have been viewed as ritual objects that are "symbolic of cushioning life" since "life can be cushioned if there is communication, if there is rapport, if there is building of their [the couple's] love together." The U.S. Bishops' Committee for Pastoral Research and Practice observes that the bride offers a bouquet to the Blessed Virgin Mary "as a personal surrender to the Virgin Mary and as a request for her protection during their entire married life." Several sources concur that the *libro y rosario* represent the importance of prayer for Christian marriage and family living.[8]

Diverse interpretations have been offered for other elements of Mexican-American marriage rites. One pastoral minister has stated that the *velo* "emphasizes the union between both spouses," while others suggest that the veil symbolizes both the chastity of the bride and, when placed over the shoulder of the groom, the couple's call to mutual fidelity in marriage. Although several observers agree that the *lazo* is an outward sign of the sacramental union between husband and wife, others add that it also signifies the "yoke of marriage." Many practitioners of the *arras* rite state that it represents the care that spouses will take to ensure that their home prospers, but at least one pastoral theologian claims that the *arras* mean the couple will share everything mutually. Some Mexican Americans point out that the thirteen coins comprise a baker's dozen, which they perceive as a ritual proclamation of the hope for prosperity. Yet others recall in the thirteen coins the presence of Christ and the twelve apostles strengthening the couple in their marital commitment.[9]

While not exhaustive, this exposition illuminates the multivalent symbolic world of Mexican-American marriage celebrations. The plurality of interpretations outlined here demonstrates that conversations with practitioners in local communities of faith, particularly couples preparing for marriage, are essential for pastoral ministers who seek to foster and enrich the celebration of marriage with Mexican-American communities.

PASTORAL GUIDELINES

As with any community of faith, the starting point for preparing a wedding liturgy with Mexican Americans is knowing and respecting their religious traditions. Mexican-American theologians have observed that the rites and practices that comprise their people's symbolic world reinforce the people's ethnic identity and even function "as a defense and protest against the demands of the dominant culture."[10] While reinforcing ethnic identity is not the primary purpose of liturgy, disregarding a people's treasured expressions of faith seriously diminishes the celebration of marriage and other sacraments.

Consulting with the couple and others involved in wedding liturgies can mutually enrich their faith expressions and the sacramental life of the church. Mexican-American practitioners enhance the Roman rite with faith expressions that are festive, sensual, familial, and deeply rooted in their history and culture. Pastoral ministers in turn can enhance the people's faith expressions through conversations that examine those practices in the light of the Gospel and the Church's liturgical tradition.

One concrete means to do this is through instruction on the historical origins of Mexican-American marriage practices. For many couples and their families, even the brief historical overview presented in this chapter would provide sufficient background for a deeper appreciation of these practices. Study of the extant marriage documents from the Iberian peninsula would also be helpful. Given the flexibility of the marriage rite, perhaps couples could select some of these texts for incorporation into the liturgy, such as the following Visigothic prayer to accompany the *arras* rite:

May your life together be like the fragrance of the lilies,
that your minds might rise easily to heaven at all times.
May you remain true, with God's help,
to the exchange of *arras* you have made
that they might be signs of united hearts
and that you might be the parents of virtuous children.[11]

Another way to enhance Mexican-American marriage practices is through critique of these practices in light of contemporary Christian reflection on the sacrament of marriage. In particular, the mutuality between the partners could be more clearly reflected in the exchange of ritual objects like the *arras*. One couple I know used the *arras* symbol, but did not like the implication that the husband was to be the breadwinner while the wife worked at home (especially since both were going to work outside the home, at least for the initial stages of their marriage). Because of this concern, they substituted their own invocation for the presentation of *arras:*

Groom:
Receive these coins as a symbol of the effort the two of us will make to live a simple life in the imitation of Christ and the Gospel.

Bride:
I receive them as a symbol of the care the two of us will take to share our goods with the poorest ones we encounter on our way.[12]

When this invocation or a similar one is used, I suggest that the bride and groom exchange *arras* rather than the groom giving them and the bride receiving them. The exchange of *arras* further mediates the ritual expression of mutuality in the Christian household. This mutuality could also be expressed by other adaptations to Mexican-American wedding ceremonies: the presentation of the *libro y rosario* to both the bride and the groom, the participation of the groom in the bouquet offering, and, as was previously mentioned, the incorporation of the groom into the entrance procession.[13] These changes clarify that the bride is not being "given" away and that the couple shares a common responsibility for the life of prayer in their family and home.

Numerous further adaptations are possible. Like the Roman rite itself, Mexican-American marriage rites continue to evolve.

Our long history of incorporating local customs into the wedding liturgy induces us to accompany Mexican-American (and other) faith communities as they shape marital celebrations; our Christian tradition impels us to enrich those celebrations by accentuating the sacramental character of the marital liturgy and covenant.

Notes

1. German Martínez, "The Newly Revised Roman Rite for Celebrating Marriage," *Worship* 69 (March 1995) 127-142; Kenneth W. Stevenson, *To Join Together: The Rite of Marriage* (New York: Pueblo, 1987) 151-153; Anscar J. Chupungco, *Liturgies of the Future: The Process and Methods of Inculturation* (Mahwah, N.J.: Paulist, 1989) 147-149.

2. Bishops' Committee for Pastoral Research and Practice, National Conference of Catholic Bishops, *Planning Your Wedding Ceremony* (Washington, D.C.: United States Catholic Conference, 1990) 11-13.

3. The description of Mexican-American marriage celebration in this section is based on Virgilio P. Elizondo, *Christianity and Culture: An Introduction to Pastoral Theology and Ministry for the Bicultural Community* (San Antonio: Mexican American Cultural Center Press, 1975) 192; *Faith Expressions of Hispanics in the Southwest* (San Antonio: Mexican American Cultural Center Press, 1979; revised 1990) 25-27; Rosa María Icaza, "Prayer, Worship, and Liturgy in a United States Hispanic Key," in *Frontiers of Hispanic Theology in the United States*, ed. with an introduction by Allan Figueroa Deck (Maryknoll, N.Y.: Orbis, 1992) 147; Raúl Gómez, Heliodoro Lucatero, and Sylvia Sánchez, *Gift and Promise: Customs and Traditions in Hispanic Rites of Marriage/Don y promesa: costumbres y tradiciones en los ritos matrimoniales hispanos* (Washington, D.C.: Instituto de Liturgia Hispana and Portland: Oregon Catholic Press, 1997).

4. Pedro I. Rovalo y equipo de la Comisión Episcopal de Liturgia, *Ritual completo de los sacramentos: textos litúrgicos oficiales aprobados para México* (Mexico City: Buena Prensa, 1976) 248-249. Quotation is author's translation of text.

5. Stevenson, *To Join Together* 45-49; Stevenson, *Nuptial Blessing: A Study of Christian Marriage Rites* (New York: Oxford University Press, 1983) 47-58; John K. Leonard, "Rites of Marriage in the Western Middle Ages," in *Medieval Liturgy: A Book of Essays*, ed. Lizette Larson-Miller (New York and London: Garland, 1997) 183-188; Mark Searle and Kenneth W. Stevenson, *Documents of the Marriage Liturgy* (Collegeville: The Liturgical Press, 1992) esp. 117, 120-121, 139; Isidore of Seville, *De ecclesiasticis officiis*, as cited in ibid., 118-119.

6. Stevenson, *Nuptial Blessing* 58-62; Robert Ricard, *The Spiritual Conquest of Mexico: An Essay on the Apostolate and the Evangelizing Methods of the Mendicant Orders in New Spain, 1523-1572*, trans. Lesley Byrd Simpson (Berkeley: University of California Press, 1966) 110-115; "Relación de Totolapa y su partido," as cited in John M. Ingham, *Mary, Michael, and Lucifer: Folk Catholicism in Central Mexico* (Austin: University of Texas Press, 1986) 24.

7. See, e.g., Abbé [Emanuel] Domenech, *Missionary Adventures in Texas and Mexico: A Personal Narrative of Six Years' Sojourn in Those Regions*, trans. from French (London: Longman, Brown, Green, Longmans, and Roberts, 1858) 259.

8. Victoria Pastrano, M.C.D.P., as cited in Pamela J. Edwards, "Ropes, Cushions and Coins: Symbols at Hispanic Weddings," *Today's Catholic* (14 June 1991) (first two quotations); Bishops' Committee for Pastoral Research and Practice, *Planning Your Wedding Ceremony* 12; Gómez, Lucatero, and Sánchez, *Gift and Promise* 8; Pastrano and John Medina, as cited in Edwards, "Ropes, Cushions and Coins." *Today's Catholic* is the archdiocesan newspaper published in San Antonio, Texas.

9. Father Alejandro Miret, as cited in Armando Fernández, "Algo viejo, algo nuevo, algo azul y algo hispano," *Vista* (June 1995) 12 (first quotation); *Faith Expressions of Hispanics in the Southwest* 26 (second quotation); Gómez, Lucatero, and Sánchez, *Gift and Promise* 5-11; Medina and Pastrano, as cited in Edwards, "Ropes, Cushions and Coins"; Elizondo, *Christianity and Culture* 192. *Vista* is the monthly magazine of the *San Antonio Express News*. First quotation is author's translation of text.

10. Ricardo Ramirez, "Liturgy from the Mexican American Perspective," *Worship* 51 (July 1977) 296. See also the second essay in this collection.

11. *Liber Ordinum*, as cited in Searle and Stevenson, *Documents of the Marriage Liturgy* 125. This book is the best English-language source for studying Iberian marriage documents.

12. Wedding of Carmen Yvette Alvarez and Victor Campos, All Saints Church, Manassas, Virginia, 14 December 1991. Quotation is author's translation of text.

13. For further suggestions on adapting the *arras* rite and other elements of Mexican-American marriage celebrations, see *Faith Expressions of Hispanics in the Southwest* 26; Edwards, "Ropes, Cushions and Coins"; Gómez, Lucatero, and Sánchez, *Gift and Promise* 12-18.

Conclusion

Even in the liturgy, the Church has no wish to impose a rigid uniformity in matters which do not implicate the faith or the good of the whole community; rather does she respect and foster the genius and talents of the various races and peoples. Anything in these peoples' way of life which is not indissolubly bound up with superstition and error she studies with sympathy and, if possible, preserves intact. Sometimes in fact she admits such things into the liturgy itself, so long as they harmonize with its true and authentic spirit.

—Vatican II, *Sacrosanctum Concilium* #37 (1963)

We must see to it that the liturgy and the common people's piety cross-fertilize each other . . . the religion of the people, with its symbolic and expressive richness, can provide the liturgy with creative dynamism. When examined with proper discernment, this dynamism can help to incarnate the universal prayer of the Church in our culture in a greater and better way.

—Latin American bishops, Puebla Conclusions #465 (1979)

Through the liturgical life of a local church, Christ, the light and salvation of all peoples, is made manifest to the particular people and culture to which that Church is sent and in which she is rooted. The Church is catholic, capable of integrating into her unity, while purifying them, all the authentic riches of cultures.

—*Catechism of the Catholic Church* #1202 (1992)

The essays in this collection explore foundational Mexican-American faith expressions and promote the celebration of these expressions in parish liturgical life. This approach to liturgical ministry is rooted in contemporary ecclesial documents that state that liturgy and a people's expressions of faith can be harmonized, integrated, and even cross-fertilize one another. While not offering a comprehensive program for liturgical ministry, this volume highlights the importance of examining the symbolic world which underlies a local community's treasured rituals and devotions. It also offers concrete examples of how these rituals and devotions can be incorporated into sacramental celebrations.

These concrete examples of how the sacraments and a people's faith expressions can mutually enrich one another could easily be multiplied, particularly for the celebration of the Sunday Eucharist and other feasts. In Hispanic communities, for example, the practice of children, parents, and grandparents blessing one another could be incorporated into the closing blessing, perhaps on special occasions like Mother's Day or Father's Day. Particular artistic expressions like the Guatemalan *nacimiento* (nativity scene) could be part of art and environment in the appropriate liturgical season. Practitioners of the home altar tradition could be invited to assist in art and environment on an ongoing basis. Devotion to the saints could be incorporated by encouraging that the people's saint images be used for art and environment on All Saints Day. The Hispanic penchant for processions could be drawn on for ordinary Sunday worship and especially for feasts such as Palm Sunday, Holy Thursday, and Corpus Christi. Further examples abound and are best learned from the cultural and religious traditions in a local community. In all instances, the desire is to enhance the understanding and celebration of the sacraments and the people's faith expressions, uniting the community in a collective act of faith and worship.

The primary concern in integrating a people's faith expressions with the liturgy is not external religious practices, however, but the world view which underlies them. Careful study can reveal elements of this world view; nonetheless, it is in celebrating the sacraments and a people's faith expressions that we more fully perceive their deeper significance and meaning. Paul VI taught that, while at times popular piety mediates distorted and even superstitious appropriations of Christianity, it also manifests a thirst for God, fosters generosity and heroic sacrifice, increases awareness of God's constant presence and love, and engenders evangelical values like patience, detachment, devotion, openness to others, and a sense of the cross in daily life (*Evangelii Nuntiandi* #48, 1975). Consistent with his approach to understanding popular piety, this volume examines not only external practices but also the interior attitudes embodied in Mexican-American rituals and devotions for celebrations such as marriage, *las posadas*, Guadalupe, Good Friday, and Ash Wednesday. While the analysis of Mexican-American foundational faith expressions offered here is by no means exhaustive (nor could it be), it provides a model for how pastoral ministers can study the faith expressions of a local community within their historical and contemporary context, learn from celebrating those expressions with a faith community, and then place them in dialogue with the Church's liturgical tradition.

Pastoral ministers can initiate this dialogue with those preparing to celebrate marriage or other sacraments and with practitioners of faith expressions like the *posadas*. In this regard, the indigenous prayer leaders recognized by local communities are particularly important. We must remember that we do not bring the faith to local communities, but join communities that already have their own leaders and means of expressing faith. A good first question to ask about our parish or faith community is, "Who are the leaders of this people's life and worship?" This does not necessarily mean clergy, catechists, liturgical coordinators, or other designated ministers. Frequently those recognized as "pastors" by the local community do not have official titles. Conversations with a local community's natural leaders enable pastoral agents to appreciate a community's life and worship, celebrate the people's treasured expressions of faith, and offer reflections on these faith expressions based on knowledge of Scripture, liturgical and sacramental theology, and the pastoral agent's own life of faith.

While centuries old, the mutual enrichment between liturgy and other expressions of faith is still a frequently untapped resource for communal worship. Those of us who are experiencing and developing this mutual enrichment find it prayerful, fascinating, and exciting. Our integrative approach to liturgical ministry allows us to celebrate the rituals we love in a new way, forging a dynamic *mestizaje* (mixture) between our rich liturgical tradition and our people's treasured expressions of faith. In our experience, this *mestizo* approach to worship can evoke lively, fervent, embodied prayer, mediating a vibrant sense of the sacred and a vivid encounter with Christ. We invite our readers to join us and employ this approach for worship with their own faith communities. Although we still have much to learn, we can attest that the creative interplay between liturgy and a people's faith expressions invigorates and revitalizes common prayer. It is not just through study but primarily through celebrating with local communities that the full potential of this creative interplay is illuminated. In the process we are enriched in our ministerial call to know and foster the Church's liturgical tradition, celebrate and enhance our people's faith expressions, and, above all, love the community of faith that we serve and accompany in worship.